SWEEPING OUT

EDWIN MORGAN

Sweeping out the Dark

CARCANET

First published in 1994 by
Carcanet Press Limited
208-212 Corn Exchange Buildings
Manchester M4 3BQ

A CIP catalogue record for this book
is available from the British Library
ISBN 1 85754 072 7

The publisher acknowledges financial assistance
from the Arts Council of Great Britain

Set in 10 pt Palatino by Bryan Williamson, Frome
Printed and bound in England by SRP Ltd, Exeter

Saryn' na kichku!

Vasily Kamensky

Lies nicht mehr – schau!
Schau nicht mehr – geh!

Paul Celan

Acknowledgements

Some of these poems have appeared in *Agenda, Chapman, New Writing, Illuminations, Spectrum, Sport, Poetry Review, Gallimaufry, Glasgow Herald, Verse, The Listener, Interference, Edinburgh Review, Numbers, Lallans, Translation & Literature, Cencrastus, New Hungarian Review*, and *Scottish Slavonic Review*. The three poems by Leopardi were published in *Leopardi: A Scottis Quair* (Edinburgh University Press, 1987), 'Eros' and 'Head' in *Of Eros and of Dust* (Oscars Press, 1992), 'Revolving Restaurant' in *Three Scottish Poets* (Canongate, 1992), 'Las Vegas' in *Under Cover* (Mainstream, 1993), and 'Sedona' in *The Five Toons Festival Collection* (Banff and Buchan District Council, 1993). The poems from *Hold Hands Among the Atoms* were published by Mariscat Press in 1991.

Contents

Red Flag Down

Who is going to praise those crowing
over the lowering? Almost everyone
it seems, forgetting snails, dimheads,
the lumpen with eyes like chuckies. Come now,
it's a red rag the bull has seen through,
saunters past. Any flared nostrils
breathe out a hubris of supersession,
nothing crude – anger, regret – no thanks.
Sodruzhestvo beats frankincense
into Boney Yeltsin's cocked hat,
heads on a salver are ten a penny,
let the hordes yell. Has he his arm
tucked into his tunic yet? No tunic?
A double-breasted suit will do.
We're democrats from Lisbon to –
to – Ulan Bator, where it's horses
currycombing the lower chamber,
throwing stirrups over khans –
oh yes, and you'll see stranger things,
winter's tales, tempests of hurry,
a suitcase with an old dog-
ma hurled into the willing Vol-
ga like an apple in a ha-
ha. Hah! A steamy, seamy time,
skew-whiff for *mesteremberek*,
brilliant for peddlers in shop-doorways,
deadly for grannies with ice-cracked bones.
What a jangling from the bell-tower.
Switch it off, let's hear the year
slipping through the bars of the moon
to thud and wail on our filthy snow.
Who will look after it? Someone. They stand,
the patient, in their queues, with nerves
of iron and will come through, right through.

Trajectory (Six Sonnets)

The Burn

We knew we had to rev and rev and drive
right through the sunset, not for pots of gold
but only, while we throbbed there in the hold,
to let the nose-cone preen itself alive
in a shimmer of lemon, orange, opal,
before it had to grow those colours, glow
those colours, groan those colours, undergo
its Shostakovich shriek of heat and shrapnel
particle-pitted from the pain of suns
that never set and wars that never end,
photographed by remote control in all
the beauty of a summer twilight, once,
before we gave the shiner leave to blend
with grit and rust and dark and love and gall.

The Blue Ring

It was not eternity the other night
I saw, but the blue ring around the globe;
the hidden seething and raving had a robe
that bonded them with what eternal light
might well be like, for all that it was blue.
The curve went over, over Vaughan's grave
in the darkness, and over wave on wave
of continents, dappled, dappling, old, new.
To sense the ball of earth alone unhung
on any golden chain, unarmed by more
than air, made it much more than dear,
as if the glimmer of the ring was flung
about an aspiration to explore
vulnerablest things devoid of fear.

The Revolution

A made world; an artifice; shiny, spooked:
in the right light you could actually see through it.
The right light was rare; well they knew it!
They believed in grin and go; hook, don't get hooked.
Bread and circuses, unbelievable; helicopters, flumes.
Satyagraha? You have only to ask.
Millions were still content to grunt and bask
in designer spas, pink jacaranda rooms
run up a moment before, out of nothing. Power
bursting all round like drunken sonic booms
for those who had ears to hear – earwax took
most of that. We teased their sleazy code, our
drills went in and gouged the viscous looms
they'd programmed. It's the earth, green. Smell! Look!

The Thesis

Those were the lazy days, the wavy days
of grass, and wisps of smoke from picnic fires.
You'd hear faint rain on leaves, no hissing tyres.
Sheep grazed abandoned atriums, a maze
of cats had scratched the porter's yucca bare.
Balsa canoes swished through the meadowsweet
down where the river met the dolphin's street.
The porter snored, or jogged in the sea air.
A broken music-box from the old times
played half a tune, played half; the rest
hovered absently among the hum
and cigarettes of the card-players. 'More limes!'
they cried. The cordial passed its test.
The boy wound and rewound, the box was dumb.

3

The Antithesis

The bands that roamed the underpass were shaggier,
the chutzpah-flaunting palace-squatters headier,
the chainsaw chandlers' caravans road-readier,
the jackets of the would-be guards were baggier.
The fit, the bad, the bold were mercenaries
with starry bedroll and a wad of banknotes.
Zombies in camouflage commanded bhang-boats,
crewing the hold with burnt-out missionaries.
Satellite anchormen were never silkier,
marathon-runners kept in step, broke bridges,
amazons cut a ball from every braggart.
But phosphorescent seas were never milkier,
fantastic sunsets burnished shell-ripped ridges,
a sculptor slapped with joy his marble blackguard.

The Synthesis

A few scarred capsules crouch in the museums
movingly, unmoving, silent, their history
upon them, their voice under the clerestory
of a wall of science giving no Te Deums
but Te Hominem, Te Hominem, right on,
as children file past the dry captions. I
circle, watching. Mostly oceans slide by.
I know the body of the ship once shone
and now we're black and shark-rough and singed red,
hah! something to pollute a rainbow if
we saw one and pushed through its pretty arc.
No promises! Hell can be ahead.
In backstreet Naples, under her living cliff,
a woman vigorously sweeps out the dark.

A Third Epitaph on an Army of Mercenaries*

We write our own; no one does it for us.
Only those who have been there know the score.
The pay was good, but thousands more before us
Would testify note-counting's but a chore.

Adrenalin, adrenalin that courses
Along the blood as bullets do's the key.
Shouts, cracks, burning buildings were the sources
Of the hot joy that made us die – or dee.

* after Housman and MacDiarmid

Three Instamatic Poems

Glasgow 15 June 1990

Nosing greyly up the Clyde on a calm summer evening
a frigate and its tug make a faint skein of ripples
and are reflected
(like trees on the bank and clouds above)
in lazy estuary pewter.
Unlazily, a man with an air-gun
has fired at HMS Plymouth to give her
a Scottish welcome; on the bridge
a figure clutches his stomach. The frigate,
having survived four bombs in the Falklands,
finds out not everyone loved that war.

New York State July 1990

A man fishing an upstate reservoir
has caught a sleeping-bag, opened it,
starts back in horror, stared at
by a livid body with strangle-marks.
Young, stocky, lapped by waters
that did not need to drown him
he has come thousands of miles to die.
The American fisherman tries to piece together
three tattoos, right arm, right breast, right leg:
a SCOTLAND THE BRAVE flag,
a spiky thistle,
a jester.

Cape Town June 1990

A storm-grounded trawler wallows on rocks.
Deep in its refrigerated hold
officials poke torches as a stack
of fifty neatly zipped-up body-bags
is carefully unzipped to show each,
like a pupa, hiding a rockhopper penguin,
stiff, cold and beautiful, with its perky ear-tuft,
stopped on its journey to a Tokyo chophouse
or to the taxidermist's stuffing-chamber.

The Lost Mandate

(Channel 4 *Comment*, July 1987)

I'd like in these few minutes to trace
The history of the recent case
Of the vanished mandate. England expects
That what its electorate elects
Shall shut its ears to every Scot
Who never voted what he's got.
Somewhere up there, there's disaffection?
It doesn't even need correction.
Forelock-tuggers to a soul,
Fillers of Labour's begging-bowl!
But still, a mandate would be handy
To brandish at dear Jock and Sandy
In case some Caledonian spark
Should lay his hand upon the ark
Of Union. Right. But could they find it,
That mandate? *Some*body had signed it,
Empire-builders countersigned it,
But two world wars had undermined it,
Poets and patriots consigned it
To built-in obsolescence. Behind it,
Before it disappeared, the wrists
Of tattered constitutionalists
Shot from their angry cuffs – no use,
It's gone! Something feels strange, feels loose.
It can't be federalism, can't be separation.
Everyone knows we are only one nation.
Maybe it's that old Scottish Assembly –
A pipe dream, like a northern Wembley.
But still the government were worried.
The mandate must be found. They hurried
The reorganization of MI5,
Grilled every shredder-owner (I've
Never seen such fearful flutter),
Probed each lake, loch, drain, and gutter,
Gave the SAS a bounty
If they could pinpoint the county
Where rumours gathered thick and fast
That here mandate was noticed last.

The Scottish Secretary chose a-
n anorexia nervosa
To slip from the unwanted scene,
While his Shadow with chagrin
Found not everyone believed him
When he said that though it grieved him
To be a Shadow, he and his chaps
Now had the mandate, under wraps,
And would reveal it bit by bit
In Westminster's rowdy pit.

Meanwhile, the Scots began to think
(God, that was moving near the brink!).
A poet and an engineer
Built a new mandate, brought it near
The Border where it was well seen,
A large, handsome, thoughtful machine
Which moved quite firmly up and down
The dales, dropping ideas, a town,
A hangar, canals, and determinations
That those who wished should still be nations.

Dido

Well is it called the shades.
You cannot imagine any grey
unknown to us, from almost black
to almost white, but never black
or white, never anything so clear.
We glide through the scrub and kick up
nothing but a little listless dust
that sinks at once exhausted or vanishes
into crowding groves, mildewed elms
one time, oaks another, nothing lasts
or keeps its shape, you might well ask
what shape a shade has. I myself
seem now to have neither age nor date.
I was thirty-five when I lay on the pyre,
but I have looked down, bleak as a crone, at
withered arms, and sometimes I have run
like the girl of twenty I once was on Sidon sands,
a girl of twenty with grey hair and grey hands.

If there is any purpose, it must be humiliation.
If there is no purpose, we must be plunged
into the roots of confusion and disorder
like a rout of atoms, to turn there, drift there,
never sleep, never eat, never cry there,
stepping the grey ways without rest,
persuaded that the maze is still a quest.

I was Queen of Carthage, am Queen of Carthage,
held our new jewel on the brow of Africa,
new city, Kirjath-Hadeshath, great construct
with its battlements forcing the promontory to stare
out toward Italy and the barbarous north.
What a transplant, what an offloading
of Phoenicians: we took Tyre and Sidon with us,
masons, soldiers, dancers, scribes, runners,
whole fishing-fleets and master traders with sails
of purple and red and banks of well-fed oarsmen,
and bankers too and treasurers, for who
had our wealth, who had our business – Egypt,

10

Babylon, musty camel-dung empires? Greece,
handless introverts? Italy, lotus-eating Etruscans
with a death-wish? No, things move west, move west.
Something might come of Italy, I admit,
if only they had a capital like Carthage, but
how can they ever catch up? Our galleys
have undone their corded bales in Britain.
We'll find Atlantis yet. Storms and fogs
are meat and drink. And what's beyond Atlantis?
Kingdoms of gold and obsidian? Rumoured trade-winds?
Kirjath-Hadeshath will chaffer water for sand,
sand for water. Without us the world
would snore with blankets up to its chin.
(And who supplied the blankets even then?)

But what good does it do the dead
to boast of a life that will never return?
I had half my days, and ended them.
It was not easy to die. I was inexpert
with the sword, fell on it at an angle,
and although it went through me, I lay twisting
like a stuck insect, tried not to groan,
did groan, so long it seemed, until many
came running and exclaiming through the palace.
When they turned me over and wrenched the blade out
I shrieked – I could not help it, great gods, I know
it was ignoble, unqueenly – but found
my spirit had still not slipped out with the bronze.
They tried to stanch the wound, made me drink wine
(I knew it was wrong, but I could not struggle),
and then as night drew on, the gods allowed me
to shiver beyond control, and leave the world.
At the last it was a crooked wall-lamp, dripping,
that I saw, and not my lover's face.

                                        Aeneas,
did you think I'd go on living, with you gone?
Did you really think that? If you did,
what use is love? Do you know what love is?
Not slinking away with your fleet in secret,
or making promises you never meant to keep,
or trailing lies about your father on your back

as you saved him from Troy in flames –
Troy that was razed four hundred years before.
You were always an adventurer, plausible,
a well-tongued Phrygian pirate, off to conquer
Italy and put the Etruscans in their urns.
Were we doomed courting in those light racy plosions
of the Greek we had to make our lingua franca?
You scorned Phoenician, I thought your Pelasgian
sounded like raking leaves from gravel paths.
No, no. Nothing was doomed that way –
nothing was doomed that I can remember –
I thought I had bound you to me so willingly –
as you me – caught in that thunderstorm,
the two of us running into the cave, you
with your floppy Phrygian cap tied under your chin
like an old washerwoman, and I almost laughed
but did not dare to, yet, and I untied it
and let it drop, untied everything, and we lay
in a nest of clothes and moss and grasses,
safe in those arms of rock, safe in love,
while the world drummed down and hissed outside.
You can never say I was not your bride.

Your second bride: all right; we've both been married,
you were forty or near it, your teenage son
was always glooming around, that little prude
and prurient with it, he's rubbish. I mean it.
You think I could ever mother that slippery eel?
He can go to – Thrace. It was you I wanted,
not your family, not your gods, I wanted
to have your child, if you had wanted it,
but you always pulled out – is that another
Pelasgian trick? – and left me aching and empty.
I had so much love I could not believe
that you had less, until your ship took off.
Ashtoreth loosed her bolt then; Melkart laughed;
Dagon dragged monsters through the gulf; Baal-Hammon
crashed his flail, I was chaff, I was blown away.
My pyre made Carthage's dark night like day.
Ash turned the sea, your rigging, even your helmet, grey.

12

Why did you go, and leave me to that fire?

You had a duty. The god told you this.

Remember me, our gods.
Remember me, our people.
Remember how I went down
indignant but truly not
unforgiving as the horizon
sail flagged me to the shades.

Stein on Venus

A crater on Venus is to be named
after Gertrude Stein.
(New item, 1991)

Where I stand, there I reign.
What is not subject is objectless.
Who knows how far my train of skirts
skirts other craters, on their knees
without evening or morning? When it is
there could ever be an end to power
I do not need to stride to tell you
or straddle a rock with a slap or scoop
fistfuls of dust to stiffen the sift –
it is all time down the red drain
to me, planted here in full pluck,
my grizzle bald as a dollar, set,
I said set, and who is going to move me?
– Only the great god Venus who
dibbled me into the rubble, saying
Water yourself! He laughed and left,
but trails his grim throne still, I know,
without servants, through sulphur, over slag,
endlessly I would say. Who loves him?
Some are standing stones, like me.
Some lie flat as dolmens. All
wait for nothing but the hiss of storms,
the crimson seething, the particle clatter,
the lightning-shattered smog of ochre,
the settling down and the rising up,
the impregnated immobilities!
God of the sun and ash, I take you
as you take me, I breathe, I sweat,
I dash my invisible waves as every
stone does, squeezing its roused seas
up and out as if they could find
beaches of meanest marram long dreamed.

14

Eros

Of course I want you up here, you can make it.
It's been so long and I'm so cold. The wind
sweeps across the Circus with rain in it,
lashes me till I'm streaming, what protection
do you think this wisp of drape is? Worse,
I'm tarnishing from the sharp traffic fumes
when all I want to do is shine and shine,
point my bow off and out and hit it –
what? – anything and anyone that loves
a flash of gleaming chest and a wingspread
as natural and as supernatural
as if I'd dropped among you at that instant
and not a hundred years ago, in my
not quite eternal youth. I'm helmeted
with messages that pulse far over London.
What I transmit I receive, the love you send me,
of course you do, all of you, I feel it
throbbing and crackling through my aluminium.
I am six feet tall. I want to be embraced.
I long for you to climb up here beside me,
twine your legs about me, clasp my neck,
press close to my good looks and kiss me so
that everyone can see, that none can doubt it.
Watch the fountain. You are almost there. See
I am totally ready for my lover.
He will jump on me, warm, thighs, arms,
lastly lips – and that will be my happiness,
in the midst and thunder of the city.

Head

At four he nudged me. At five I exploded
in his mouth. At six I had a pizza,
coffee, glass of house red. At
seven I boarded the sunset bus
west in a warm blaze. At eight
I had an image: it flickered eagerly
as I moved from room to room and
got me sitting at my table to watch it
settle: I watched it settle and took
its signal and though the bus had brought me
through an 'evening of extraordinary
splendour and beauty' I have nothing
to write of that or of wine. At nine
I had the image of his face in focus
shining slightly in the half-light
as he raised it from his task
and in profile gave a sudden grin,
his open lips still joined by two
glistening sticky threads like tiger's
teeth he slowly watching me
took his hand and wiped away.

At twelve, but three nights later, I
brought that head back here for all.

Taormina

The Baron has disposed the flesh.
It's fixed to say his every wish.

Bright light falling hard and hot
Gives the lens its sultry lot.

A broken column makes a seat
For swarthy Carlo, nude and neat.

Enrico holds a flying-fish
And stuffs his finger in, the bitch!

Paolo and Pietro loll on rocks
In headbands only, chewing stalks.

A straw hat keeps Tommaso cool.
He's furnished heavy, long and full.

Cicada fields take Marco's flute
And thick black hair and shepherd's foot.

Lorenzo is half decent in
A tunic and a winning grin.

The agave and the prickly pear
Back up Vincenzo's brazen stare.

With hip thrust out, and artless pout,
Giovanni's still a sturdy lout.

Sicilian midday; the sun steeps
The lizard's slab; Luigi sleeps

And lies as perfectly exposed
As German shutter can disclose.

These youths are kitsch, not camp, said Barthes.
You gaze, but cannot take their part.

The ivy trails, the olive burns.
Late shadows mould the courtyard urns.

In Memoriam Laura Riding

Not cursory, flashes probed a row of roofs
To plant best thunder in, grey-black roots
Watered with instant storm. Darkening rooms
Heard dogs howl. Weathermen cast runes.

Towns were darker than rooms very quick.
In a hullabaloo suddenly light quit.
Nature chewed its twister like a quid,
Spat out black wreckage with the merry quip

It keeps for admonition. Batten down,
You're going up! A homestead like a dhow
Sails through high dusty air. No doubt
Some vanish, crash, cry. Some are to drown,

Tornadoes whisper as they scrub them with wind,
Wash them off, run with them, leave them no wish.
Florida tucks language under her wing,
Waits for wet true sun, the soar of will.

It's all right that the sounds have broken loose.
It's all right that there are no rhymes left.
It's all right to see off the last metaphor,
Silent, watchful, in the eye of the hurricane.

It is all right, all of it is right.
Even that it is not in this poem either,
Laura, the truth, is all right. The real tree
Stands – just there – with the rain-drops on it.

dsh: recollection of a vortex

a swirling cloak on great western road
a swirling monk filling the lift
a swirling head in drifts of coffee
a swirling hand of divagations
a swirling book of onionskins
a swirling show of spacedout typestracts
a swirling skirt blown on my balcony
a swirling eye makes traffic sacred
a swirling far goodbye is echoed
a swirling and a far good
a swirling and a good eye
a swirling going surely by

Translated from a Tablet in
the Royal Library at Nineveh
For Robert Cummings at 50

On my fiftieth [birthday] I received in audience

    The Nabatean Ambassador and his consort[s]
    A satrap of Bactria
    The Dowager [of the] Hanging Gardens
    The King of Sheba
    Ms Sappho and her P[leiades?]
    The Eleusinian [team?]
    The blind Astronomer-Royal of Babylon
    The Spartan Plenipotentiary and his ephebe
    The Baker of the [rolls?]
    The Librarian and her oven-[minder?]
    A [.....] of b[.....]s

I was given [presents] as under

    50 camels with appurtenances
    1 [wine-]skin [drawn by] four oxen
    1 [set] whale[-bone] chess[men]
    1 Phrygian cap
    1 T[r?]oy[an] horse
    5 Egyptian virgins [?]
    2 stoned date-[bearers?]
    4 wheels
    1 Persian boy
    1 jar [of] all [the] perfumes [of] Arabia
    20 buckets of [.....]
    10 [corded?] [bales?] undone
    6 chrysoprase strigils
    1 [age?] of gold

A Sonnet

For Jonathan Williams at 60

Salutations in harmonious solidarity!
With word-hoards brimming, the far-flung sodality
Of your well-wishers indent for you a totality
Of good and hale, not forgetting hilarity.
May orchids and simples grace your florality
With quincunxes of blushing clarity,
While zigzag wings bring pied fritillarity
Into the purples of reality.
May the long sung tooth in the dale of carnality
Sharpen your sagacity without disparity.
May you press the button of prestidigitality,
Pot the blague of paronomasiality,
Number the bear-droppings of particularity,
And take much joy in your sexagesimality!

Macaronicon

For Tom Scott at 75

That night I saw a moor with scattered fires.
Grey smoke drifted through to break the gleam
of weapons abandoned. Figures, call them no more,
skulked in and out of the smoke-swirls, half-crouched,
knifed any bundles that still stirred or groaned,
cut rings off to test any playing possum.
No moon, only the fires. Ane barand steid,
the flichter an the smeek, the wappins grundit,
the besy fowk like sheddas getherin there
tae pyke oot ony gliff o life, kickin
corp an hauf-corp for a tellin grane,
howkin the gowd rings, leavin the braw een
for corbies. Nuit d'un champ de misères,
petits feux partout, et la fumée qui roule
parmi les armes, les mourants et les morts,
les furtives figures qui frôlent et tuent
ces blessés, arrachant pendant le râle
doigt, anneau, joyau, vie et tout.
Et la lune s'endormit. Mi ritrovai
per uno campo oscuro che la guerra
aveva guastato, corpo sul corpo, gemito
sul gemito, fuoco sul fuoco, fumo
sul fumo, ed i furfatori infernali
robbing and hacking until the very dead
yowlit an chirmit Oh que c'est lointain
et fort, l'espoir des hommes, benigna pax!

San Diego

There's a gorgeous park in San Diego
where water-lilies shade the show
of goldfish flicking tails below.

A painter on a folding stool
tilts his block towards the pool.
He has a white hat to keep cool.

How can he catch those dragonflies?
I like how he screws up his eyes.
The lily glistens where it lies

and that won't be too hard, but coils
of waving watery stems are foils
for puckish terrapins chasing oils

across the well-stretched canvas. Let
all be caught within a net
of gold, black, green, wax-white, and set

upon a whitewashed wall at last
in a black frame, with houseplants massed
in green and gold, mortal, outclassed –

it's only miles to Mexico,
not many, if you want to know.
I roll my picture up and go.

Tijuana

Half a mile of car repair shops,
pungent dust when the bus stops,
dust where the one-legged beggar hops.

Indian women line the road
expressionless as idols, load
their trays with trinkets, bide and bode.

Their children have torn trainers though,
twitch to fizzing Sonys, know
how hawklike faces break and glow.

The eyes are black, the rags are grey,
America's an hour away,
the chico plans it night and day.

Their mothers squat in black as if
five centuries had left them stiff,
straight-backed against an unseen cliff.

Traffic rackets through the town.
Photographers with monkeys frown
at anyone who lets them down.

The beer is cold; a band strikes up;
black coffee hisses in the cup.
Circus is coming, hup, hup, hup!

Las Vegas

They crouch at handles day and night.
They crunch each mental fruit in sight.
They nurse their options through the blight.

The air-conditioning is cool.
Any found sweating is a fool,
and swearing is tales out of school.

Unstubbed cigarettes, worms of ash;
loosened tie and drooping tache;
dreams of streams of cash to stash.

What is it, moon, dawn, who cares?
Time shadows them unawares,
their teeth whistle threadbare airs.

Not hungry yet? They're thin with hope.
They glaze and twitch, but not from dope,
lay figures in an endless soap.

Outside, the sky is teatime blue.
The wet bikinis are see-through.
The pool has shrieks. Li-lo or do.

But inside, it is never late.
What you do is done by fate.
And light burns hard, inveterate.

Motel

Palm-trees sprang, high fountains sprang
between the palms, arched, splash-sang
to the splay-fronded overhang.

Bays and peninsulas, a maze
of walkways sizzling in the blaze,
a spider-crab of crooked ways

bewitched the guests and tried their feet
to master this entrenched retreat
in Arizona's pounding heat.

A cactus garden seemed its heart.
Though greener gardens played their part,
it startled as if made by art.

Hands up, six foot high, they breathed,
these prickly Galateas wreathed
in twisted smiles, with thrusts that seethed

for givers of a desert kiss –
leathered Pygmalions who'd not miss
a gouge of blood to get their bliss.

But darting humming-birds and wings
of sprinklers flashed through living things
what ordinary beauty brings.

Sedona

Rough ride up the Red Rock track!
Cram the jeep, front, sides, back!
Caps on, shades on, hang on Mac!

We grind the rubble, cloud on cloud
puffs out from ruts others have ploughed.
We bounce, we startle pines, we're loud

in the high silences we climb to.
Silence can wait, we haven't time to.
Go gently? It would be a crime to.

Shroud us, red dust, another skin.
Burn us, red sun, without, within.
Make us, red rock, your stony kin.

We look back from each hairpin bend.
The scarps have faults we'll never mend,
but what we wish can never end.

Like angels in our own whirlwind,
or brief dust-devils gathered, thinned,
gathered again, we're underpinned

by energies that make or break,
and we won't break, though bones may shake
with climbing for the climbing's sake.

Hotel

'Kneel between my legs.' Let's rhyme.
'Take it easy, take your time.
Oh god –' That's rhyming on a dime.

Flimsy curtains filter glare.
Hot whispers chafe the lifeless air.
A peeling fire-escape looms bare

beyond the window in the heat
that melts it down into the street
where sun and sticky shirt-sleeves meet.

Shimmering petrol afternoons!
Sundaes pushed by languid spoons!
Desires half-sketched like broken runes!

Lie down and let the time unfold.
Fix your horizontal hold.
Sweat out the movie if it's old

and if it's not, switch off. Screech
of wheels and howl of sirens leach
into another world. Your speech

is all of dreams, nakedness, calm.
Drowse it out and swim in balm.
'Roll over.' Californian psalm.

Revolving Restaurant

As round we go, round we go,
not like that but very slow,
we watch the whole Bay far below.

The lifted fork stands still to scan
that best of twilights made by man,
enchanted metropolitan.

The lights come on, the dark comes down,
gold winks through tufts of leafy brown,
mist-grey waters lap the town.

Bridges, banks, hotels are creeping,
brilliant, silently unsleeping,
in and out of our rapt keeping.

Look, is that London? – Not that one,
no city, but one beyond the sun –
Jack – in his boat – when day is done –

sailing well out to make a catch
beneath the stars? We'll never match
him, toying with our harmless batch

of sprouts, to muzak, or the sea
where only thoughts, wishes, can be
as round we go, and think us free.

from

Hold Hands Among the Atoms

A Departure

Before we left, we sat down like old Russians,
breathed steadily till none of us was anxious
any more, and our packed gear seemed gold-foiled
in the low sun, like gifts. We held our helmets
loose in our laps. The place had a great quietness,
the marble floor, the porch, the little fountain.
Nothing escapes from time, but it was like that.
We looked out where the universe was slanting
off and down, bright, full of forms, quite distant
but then very near and to be reached. Our captain
nodded, rose, we rose, put on our helmets.
It was vincible now, that illimitable.

Difference

The endless variousness is all for praises.
The faces, passing, never make an empire.
And Iskander stopped writing in Abkhazian,
Aigi in Chuvash, Rytkheu in Chukcha.
So much the worse, so much the worse. You think not?
You'd rather have the second-best as long as
millions get it? – Mission, you cry, the mission!
we want the mass to move en bloc, not crunch on
caltrops, inessentials, unideals!
We catch an awkward squad we do a brainwash
with promises of universal favour
far beyond the sheep-fanks, fish-holes, shamans.
Why not – it's easy – cut fish-holes in Russian?
– The endless variousness evolves, the empire
expires in frozen edicts, you can skate there
but soon you're off the edge, and then there's no one
bar the unassimilated – *bar-bar, bar-bar* –
to save you, and why should they, since you doomed them
to hold their tongue, and everything that made them
to their hearts, flags burning a locked drawer,
songs that are not alien to the alien,
accreted stinging stories mocking labials
where you are a *bar-bar* to them. The faces
pass, the individuals, how there can be such
difference we do not know but what we do know
is that an absolute instinct loves it different,
the world, the dialectic, the packed coaches
whistling at daybreak through the patched countries.

A Chapter

They thought they only wanted social justice,
but when it came they caught an unknown sickness.
Oh no there were no marks upon their bodies,
the only pain they said they felt was inward.
Their simple well-cut clothes and well-kept houses,
the well-swept streets and unpolluted highways,
the lifts that worked, the clear blue seas, graffiti
buried under harmonies of paintwork,
were not enough to save them from disfavour,
so they called it, baffled by the absence
of satisfactions they had strained their souls for.
The young ones gathered in tight knots at corners,
an older man would stare across the table
as well-cooked food grew cold, a painful dreaming
sending his spirit through his wife and children
as if they were no more than paper sketches
uselessly interposed before the terrible.
And down among the well-spaced cars and buses
at times a driver would begin to shiver,
put his whole course on automatic, waiting
for something black to fasten on the windscreen
and give him leave to crash in solid blindness.
A generation then began to perish,
wasted by longings in the well-lit cities,
drowned on white beaches where they sat abstracted,
exposed on hilltops under constellations
they strained to glimpse beneath their cloudy burden.
Yet no one knew what laws must have been broken,
or whether their malaise was good or evil.
And that was when they heard the distant shouting.

A Change

I ordered everyone to do some shouting
as we came through the last pass to the city.
Shout what you like, I said, but give it power.
Our worn accoutrements were hanging from us
like rags of the red rain-forest lichen
we'd camouflaged our stealth with when we had to,
but now we were so boisterous, I was, they were,
under high winds that tore the clouds from hiding
and drove us with them through that scrubby valley,
we'd no concealment, needed none, kept calling
backwards and forwards, imitating bird-cries,
shouting at last in unknown tongues, stumbling
unbelted, shorts about our ankles, kicked off
as we raced through the sage and got snakes scattering –
a fang could never take a joke – our laughter
happy to raise not lay the dust, the sage-brush
happy to purple not blanch flashing skin, our weapons
happy to dangle clashing unprimed but priming
our awesome advancing high-yaller charivari.

Towers and real roads, said the field-glasses
I never threw away. It was worth a crescendo
that the roads were so straight, so neat with motors.
I passed the glasses round, they must all see it.
I said we should make it just about midday.
There must be no harmony, no marching.
Each to his own. Some could be quite naked,
others swathed in vine-leaves, monkeys, leeches.
Throats could be roughened by the last bad brandy.
No one needed haranguing. We hurtled into
the outer suburbs in an hour, with cartwheels,
with shouts that I thought totally unmatchable,
with animals, with scent of sage, with kisses
blown to startled children, to forks half-lifted
behind the beautiful windows of their lunchtime.

October in Albania

White kilts and crimson jackets, curvy daggers
and cloaks that might be plaids – a whole Levant of
crypto-Scots – 'I like the Albanians much,' wrote
Byron, had himself painted in their costume.
They still remember him in new Tirana.
Rapid Albanian patter from a guide at
the ethnographic museum became luminous
as he dropped in the magic name and pointed
at dress that might have graced Scotch bards, or pashas.
Belated Sixties flares and decent shirt-sleeves
now, in the bright October heat; no daggers;
they export chrome, hydroelectric power,
tobacco, handmade carpets, rear turkeys,
stroll across carless streets with unwrapped fragrant
loaves, and stare amazed as western strangers
tilt cameras at the rooftop neon mantras –
GLORY TO THE PARTY OF LABOUR OF SHQIPËRIA

And what is Shqipëria, land of eagles?
The rebel-roasting pashas have all vanished,
partisan-hanging nazis have all vanished,
all the Zogs and all the gods have vanished.
There's neither star wars here, nor perestroika,
no Hiltons, and no Palaces of Culture,
neither Stolichnaya nor Coca-Cola.
Long narrow mountain-backboned rivery country
of gorge and gully and beach, of pines and roses,
of palms in parks and avenues and gardens
and palms where every gorgeous comb seemed perfect
high on a hill to spread their bearing beauty
over and among the unbearing tombstones
polished in horizontal row on row in
the Cemetery of the Martyrs, soldiers
and partisans of the last hitlerite years, givers
of blood for that most ancient stubborn Illyria.
And one slab, with two armed guards at attention,
a tiny red flag and a twist of flowers,
the very essence of simplicity, said
ENVER HOXHA. Mother Albania breasted

the blue clear air in stone across Tirana.
The white marble plateau was peaceful, silent.
I thought of Scotland's other, shameful silence,
and Mother Scotland like a crone in cast-offs,
breasting nothing; took the steps down, slowly.

An Island

Heavy as rum and sweeter than molasses
that island pitched its clam-shells into waters
blue and gently shelving, swum-in, sharkless.
The sticklike centenarian storytellers –
there were some three of them at easy reckoning –
invaded barbecues and lulled the feasters
(as wild pig and clam devils drowned in kava
glistened through the pores of bored teenagers)
with histories of their forefathers' heroes
drawing up war canoes on sands they reddened
with axed princes and gorging their parched throats
with wild pig and clam devils drowned in kava.
To hell with war, the young men thought, as gobbets
of gristle tickled their plump chests, and pissing
through their loin-cloths made a raucous pastime.
Unsteady girls were shrieking between hiccups.
The storytellers tottered into hammocks.
Unadmired, the never less than brilliant
stars began to prick the dark. And never
a squeak from stuck princes. A Pacific Homer
was itching strongly to be born, oh he'd be
bringing in the dead drunk, burned on fire-stones,
and high-tide-drowned slumped boys like gods, and vomit
slurped from coconuts by fuddled fathers
who retched with terror as a raw-boned morning
hit them from somewhere in the universe they
thought it was a mercy to have forgotten.

A Ceremony

Stout bollards and red cones provide corrals for
visitors of curiosity and distinction.
The bunting flies in bright but tasteful pastels.
Cool awnings wait for any faint observers.
The ritual of Trampling on the People
is annual, public, ancient, and instructive,
and draws large throngs into the Square of Squares for
reasons imaginable and unimaginable.
All traffic is forbidden, and a thousand
citizens from the peripheral favelas
lie prostrate and quite naked on the asphalt
with stiff arms by their sides. The heat beats fiercely.
A hundred of the great ones of the region,
some dripping with imperial insignia,
some plainly suited in grey polyester,
some few with masks, though that was hardly needful,
and all smart-booted, cuban-heeled, spurred, studded,
descend from their ungaudy valanced platform.
A midday cannon galvanized the phalanx
to strut along the backs the high sun offered,
crisscrossing in the carefullest formation
till none escaped the heel and the dispassion
which ground knees, bellies, nipples, lips, and foreheads
briefly into the stony earth they came from.
At a command, the tramplers regained their dais.
A further cannon-shot, and the bruised beings
stumbled erect in silence, and dispersing
into the streets and avenues with neither
clothes nor shame at lack of them, gave nature
more than human power had dispossessed there,
while jaunty music froze our very spirit
into vows that set like iron, and bound us.

A Statue

The statue was manhandled down quite slowly
for safety's sake, being so huge and heavy,
and hundreds more than had been reckoned likely
came to stare and shout and spit and cheer those
businesslike demolishers. Then they were dancing
on fallen concrete epaulettes, a shoulder,
a block of rain-black cheek where the split face had
burst and spilt no blood or brain, no anything
apart from rusty rods that mocked each human
backbone with their undestroyed reminder
of iron laws and iron men; dance! tear them!
By nightfall, all had gone. The broken pieces
lay huddled under an uneasy moonlight.
Clouds trailed their gravecloths. Shots cracked, though faintly.
One by one, muffled scuttling figures gathered
among the ruins and began to pocket fragments,
melting off quickly into the dark. None gestured,
none spoke. A knuckle, an ear-lobe, a button
vanished to unknown cupboards and shoe-boxes,
not ikons for diehards but mere mementoes
of bad times those who took them hardly dreamed of
returning, except that they did dream it, later,
making their children finger a few ugly
shards of pain that never can be buried.

Persuasion

You never thought much of the darkness, did you?
You wanted everything so open, open –
I said it could not be – you laughed, and shook me,
and pointed me and swivelled me to windows,
doors, rivers, skies – said it must be, must issue
right out if it was to have any honour –
what: love? – yes: love; it must seal up its burrow,
must take a stair or two, a flight or two, for
poles, horizons, convoys, elevations –
but tender still to backcourts and dim woodlands.
Oh, never ask where darkness is if light can
break down the very splinters of the jambs – be
sure I know you can take in the sunlight
through every pore and nothing will be blinded
or shrivelled up like moth in flame or crippled
by some excess of nakedness – just give it,
your intelligence, your faith I really mean, your
faith, that's it, to see the streets so brilliant
after gales you really can go out there,
you really can have something of that gladness,
many things under the sun, and not disheartened,
so many in their ways going beside you.

An Offer

Imagine all the sea was turned to money,
lapping the shore with notes and twinkling silver,
how many do you think would jump the pierhead,
or hire a hovercraft to waft it closer,
or drown, scrabbling with sacks through miles of paper?
The maddened gulls and guillemots are starving,
the stalled propellers vainly scrunching millions,
the submarines clank under squalls of quarters,
the blinded bathysphere has ten-pound windows.
Imagine when this wealth has turned to coral,
and banks of it rise up, as sharp as razors,
and children with unwary feet are bleeding
as they scamper on the ghosts of long-dead deutschmarks.
What would you pay to have a new convulsion
send the reefs roaring to greed-grey Avernus?

An Elegy

Nil-nisi-bonum-bloody-Hirohito,
amiable plankton dissector, never doubted
prisoners should have well-defined rib-cages,
contours not shrouded by superfluous flesh-rolls,
you had to see the slavery, it was stoic,
sunken eyes and stick legs, not statistics,
you had to hear the beaten scream, and sometimes
that faintest plump of entrails on the concrete,
large white barbarians, and so they were too
as happened, were the odds evened in ovens
of nuclear fire? Electronic gardens
and a cherry-tree and no weapons, fine now
is it? Whales to be culled only for science?
All's-well-that-ends-well-Akihito, bowing
to his father's chrysanthemums, has need of nightmares
we can only give him in poems, even
from the other side of the world, and even
from another world than this if there was one, where
shades, if there were shades, would gather singing
matters the living cannot quite yet sing of,
lacking the desolation of those dead ones.
But what we can we write, here, Hirohito.

Hands On, 1937

John S. Clarke, festooned with snakes, said, 'Touch one,
look closely, they're quite beautiful; not slimy;
come on, come down to the front now, that's better.
Don't be afraid, girls, aren't these eyes pure jewels?
Come on lads, stretch your hands out, try this johnny,
I bet it's like no creature you ever handled.'
I thought the lecture had been good, but this was
unforeseen, an unknown world, strange bonus –
the dry brown coil was at first almost leaden,
slightly rough but inert, with scales tight-fitting
like Inca walls, till what seemed a faint tickling
became a very crawling of the flesh as
movement began to test my arm, the ripples
of an almost unfathomable power
rhythmically saying, I am living:
you may not love me but oh how I am living!
And it is all one life, in tanks, bags, boxes,
lecture-theatres, outhouses, fronds of bracken,
rivers for men and serpents to swim over
from dark bank to dark bank and vanish quickly
about their business in raw grass and reedland,
scale, sole, palm, tail, brow, roving, brushing, touching.

A Dragon

We brushed out suddenly and very roughly
from the black thicket, sweating, angry, filthy,
adventurers dishevelled to our toecaps –
oh yes we had our boots, for snakes and leeches –
still trailing all that sodden gear, tents, ponchos,
machetes almost blunt with hacking, bugles
bashed and drowned and merely ornamental –
when we saw what was not an open country –
oh that would be too simple for our masters
up there, if there are any, we don't think so –
but only an incomparable garden
we gingered into with an uncouth shyness,
tugging shirts into belts, pretending order,
whistling then desisting, cut turf a wonder,
lakes, little Turkish kiosks, laurel bowers,
vetiver-scented fountains – who would dare to
break such glassy arches with the grime we'd
gathered in our trudging mangrove trances?
We stuttered down to love-seats; air was gentle;
abstraction took us one by one as listening
to a bird – unknown – sing three clear notes descending
in inhuman not sad not happy sweetness,
we sat a while like unfinished statues, knowing
our caravanserai was not for gardens.

Only later we learned there was a dragon,
often not present, always sometimes present,
not to be calculated. Papery arbours
whisper softly. Gardeners with light wheelbarrows
trundle themselves home to wife and children,
not even glancing at what must be evening
drawing dark wings high over the poplars.
But fountain jets are steam by midnight. Chaos
blows stacked bricks through the screaming cottage cradles.
Something very old is at large, breathing.
A single violet is an irritation
so intense that it is burnt to ashes,
the ashes stamped to dust, and the dust roared at

till not a particle could find its neighbour.
They say it is in pain, to cause such havoc.
We doubt it – but we are only fighters.
We should have stayed there, should have stood there,
    comrades!

An Abandoned Culvert

The daffodils sang shrill within the culvert.
Their almost acid notes amazed the darkness
culverts are happiest with. They could not cower,
the yellow birds, pure cries on stilts, conundrums
to burst the reason of those mineral courses.
Five stubborn half-fluted half-ragged non-fluting trumpets
blared the dank brickfall grit into submission.
Whatever daffodils can say, they said it
louder and sharper than the stalagmites they
might have been, if all the timorous ages
had managed to conspire against some thrusting
of the dumb seed that could not know, yet knew, it
had to unapologetically
proclaim a yellow and not golden treasure
unyielding to the kisses of the digger.

A City

– What was all that then? – What? – *That*. – That was *Glasgow*.
It's a film, an epic, lasts for, anyway
keep watching, it's not real, so everything is
melting at the edges and could go, you have to
remember some of it was shot in Moscow,
parts in Chicago, and then of course the people
break up occasionally, they're only graphics,
look there's two businessmen gone zigzag, they'll be
off-screen in one moment, yes, I thought so.
– What a sky though. – Ah well, the sky is listed,
change as it may. It's a peculiar platinum
with roary sunset flecks and fissures, rigging
was best against it, gone now, don't regret it,
move on, and if you wait you'll see some children,
oh it's a fine effect, maybe they're real, some
giant children pulling down a curtain
of platinum and scarlet stuff as airy
as it seems strong, and they'll begin to play there,
bouncing their shrill cries till it's too dark to
catch a shadow running along the backcloth,
and they still won't go home, despite the credits.
– You mean the film goes on, beyond the credits?
– You'll have to wait and see, won't you? It's worth it.
– I'm not persuaded even of its existence.
– What, *Glasgow*? – The city, not the film. – The city
is the film. – Oh come on. – I tell you. – Right then,
look. Renfield Street, marchers, banners, slogans.
Read the message, hear the chant. – Lights! Camera!
– But where are the children? – That I grant you;
somewhere, huge presences; shouting, laughter;
hunch-cuddy-hunch against a phantom housewall.

A Smokehouse

The smokehouse girl was talking to the salmon.
Go down, come up, get on that rack, my beauty.
You'll not be leaping on this smoky ladder.
Just listen to the wood-chips quietly fuming,
and oh if you could tap that barrel you'd be
swimming in the smell of sweeter forests
than any you nudged warily through reed-beds.
Money in purse is sweeter still. No poacher
will slip your rosy goldy squeeze-packed meltings
in his mouth. Receptions with a touch of lemon
will strike up, and a glass of something, burst of
well-bred strings. Swim in that, you stupid
creature! Flies have hooks when they're too perfect,
your mother must have told you. What, she didn't?
Can't you watch shadows? I think you're as greedy
as we are, even when you see the line you
snatch the lure, as if a gulp could render
the impending less terrible or fortify the present
with food that chokes on air. Keep smoking will you!
Turn that squashed eye away. I need my wages.
Who is on the rack at Achiltibuie?

Il Traviato

That's my eyes at their brightest and biggest.
It's belladonna. I've a friend who. Not that
I'd ever use too much, did once, came out of
delirium after a week of sweats, you learn. But
I'm so pale now, some men like the contrast
as I stand in the park with my eyes burning,
or glide among the poplars, they're thin as I am
but seem to manage, get their light, get nourished
as I get trade although the Wraith's my nickname.
I ought to be in bed, probably, maybe.
In any case my lover sends me out now,
he says it's all I'm good for, bring some money.
He hides my razor till I'm 'interesting',
a chalky portrait ruffed in my black stubble.
I mustn't be too hard on him. The years we.
It all comes down to what kind of constant
you believe in, doesn't it, not mathematics
but as if you had the faintest brilliance
that was only yours, not to let any sickness
douse it, or despair creeping with a snuffer.
I sometimes think I wish it could be ended
– those hard-faced brutes that hit you at the climax –
but then I go on, don't I, as everyone
should, pressing through the streets with glances
for all and everything, not to miss crumbs of
life, drops of the crowded flowing wonder.

A Pastoral

The glen, the dene, the chine, the dell, the leasowe –
a world of secrets goes about its business
and never needs to tell you until maybe
when you lie drowsing in the summer murmur
a cow snorts and a quick hoof-splinter flashes
colours and lights in the low water-meadow
and you say Oh I can't doze, I must remember.
The hoofs move and the rings break and the colours
dapple those soggy shallows so demandingly,
the big head droops and puffs and slops, shakes drops off,
trundles its bulk after it, brindling damply,
dunly happy, chewing so half-abstractedly,
you might think messages that very midday
were coming at you, but you can't remember
even though you sat up with your eyes shaded,
ants running off in panic, the smell of grasses
deliriously clovery, the sweets and greens and breathings
round you and in you, an almost silent Woodstock
where, yes that's it, throw off, you can be naked
as an ant, pick your way among not lovers
with their beads and smoke, but even closer secrets,
weeds disregarded, rainbows you must wade through.
Everything would give everything to be remembered.

Days

Where have those long days gone that used to charm us
before we knew we could be discontented?
I said the grass was waves, my toy boat bobbing.
To get the swishing sound I thought was sea was
steady tugs on the string. We made a mortal
soup then in a bent bowl, dandelions, burnwater,
curls of dropped catkins, what not else, mullocked it
about, had just the sense to sip not swallow.
Was it sun or clouds, who knows, that was for grown-ups.
We'd hours with roadmenders, their hut forbidden
and so a place of great resort, a dusty
sweaty sweary tarry magic caravan,
they quizzed us, shared their cans of tea, felt our
no muscles and laughed, surrounded us like a story
of familiar giants we'd never be afraid of.
The time that must have come and gone was faces
at windows, angry shouts from doorways, this minute,
come in, until we too could sense the shadows
advancing with what must be the end. Scliffing
the pavement, throwing burrs, they have to, slowly,
the children, come home, where all the clocks are racing.

A Needle

They'll find it in the haystack, the good needle.
The straw house may be stars rings strings eclipses
and nothing going straight can pierce the jungle
of dimensions and no expedition not carrying
time with them in a bag can hope to live through
tight-forked tick-filled random-steaming centuries
and navigators and their sons and daughters
may feel fate rather than some constellation
is stacked against them and a radioactive
hand may scrabble palsied at the panel
when ships are briefly bucked by something grimmer
than light and even though some one or two should
lock into hopeless madness and be ejected
and black religions come and go in phases
to induce despair and dazzling mathematicians
clutch at straws and smoke them and so sleepwalk:
when all is said and done it can't be hidden,
it glints among a nebula in ruins,
it holds itself among the suns, its patience
sits among the dust-clouds that can tarnish
everything less than goodness; invisible
it cannot be but long unseen and longing
to be seen: oh yes and to be used, to swoop through
wounds it would knit, banners to be invested
with futures of things known, frames to be figured
to hopes as iron as Homer's woman fed on,
against the odds of being only human.

A Vanguard

We came to the end of the world at midnight.
Someone called out from the back of the column,
Is that it then? What is it like? I answered,
Whatever you have of imagination
you must use. Come forward. All of you. Stand easy.
Through so much dust, we were no smart company,
but somehow the tired group seemed monumental
as any old stone circle where they clustered
gravely over staves and rifles and brooded
above the yelling abyss we'd reached the lip of.
And those who thought a globe could never have one –
abyss, I mean, edge, rim, sick slope to vacancy –
began to shiver at celestial mechanics
crumbling away. It must be a ravine then,
fog, darkness, the farther bank is hidden –
one of them said, using imagination.
No one believed that rational man; the spirit
of the place, our chilling sweat, the terrible groaning
from throats unseen below our feet, took toll of
any reason we had left. What had we looked for
in fact but the end of the world, we the vanguard
sent out to scotch or seal appalling rumours.
So there we were. Was it hell? We saw no one.
The cold grew more intense. Let's go back then,
I said, it's not the end of the world. Joking
broke the spell. Someone laughed. A ravine surely,
windy caves and flues like voices. And supper
a short march away. Soon they would start whistling.
I kept my thoughts, but nothing would do, nothing.
No end in time was near, or in space possible.
As for the dead, who am I to appease them,
a scout, a ragged man, a storyteller?

Aunt Myra (1901-1989)

A horse in a field in a picture is easy.
A man in a room with a fan, we wonder.
It might be whirring blades in steamy downtown –
but no, it's what she's left beside her dance-cards.
How she sat out a foxtrot at the Plaza
and fanned her brow, those far-off flirty Twenties
he opens and shuts with an unpractised gesture
that leaves the years half-laughing at the pathos
of the clumsy, until rising strings have swept them
dancing again into silence. The room darkens
with a blue lingering glow above the roof-tops
but the man still stands there, holding up the dangling
dance-cards by their tiny attached pencils.
The cords which are so light seem to him heavy
as if they were about to take the strain of
tender evenings descending into memory.
Something is hard, not easy, though it's clearly
a man, a fan, a woman, a room, a picture.

Morning in Naples

At six in the morning, in the empty side-street
I waited for the motor to the airport:
cool pigeon-whirring Sunday, early stillness
of the manic city, a white cat on the cobbles
going home, an ancient jangle from a tower
just seen, cracked wall behind cracked wall, a flourish
of indomitable weeds in the high stonework
and then the freshness, the faintly stirring silence
of the lightening blue overhead uncloudedly
arching out east to veiled Vesuvius.
The bag at my feet was perfect: all transience,
all pause, all flight, all as out of time as
the bells were out of tune, and as I stood there
watching for a white car I was not watching
for anything but a world beginning over,
over and over without a blurt of trumpets,
up from the bay sea haze with the Greek founders
until unlikely now, uneven pavement,
paw and claw on stone and peal in sunshine,
and me unsweating yet, but still uncertain
as one car seems to slow, and yes, she's waving.
I lift my bag, she stops, the spell is broken.
We sped through the no traffic. Conversation
streamed out behind us like a scarf, or banner,
or something else we were busily transferring
into an insatiable distance.

A Memorial

Stupendous days of unattended toilets!
bright eye-devouring afternoons, hesit-
ancies of dusk, rustle and whisper of midnights
where sometimes the full moon would make a sculpture
of two close heads as it worked through a grating,
or absolute eye-prickling foggy blackness
would let divine touch heal the lonely, leaven
the ugly, foreground the age-old desperations;
and locals would stroll round on sunny mornings
with dog or crossword, oh, half-honestly but
not without a flickering eye. By Kelvin waters,
by Liffey waters we watched the shadows gather,
heard those hoarse commands that were entreaties,
caught a match sputtering, cupped hands, a cheekbone,
waited timeless as the sullen flotsam
wandered below to all-receiving ocean.

Sometimes a padlocked door remains, more often
a demolished space, or emptiness refilled with
seats, a shelter, a kiosk, some trees; even
a real cottage: and the wind whistles round it.
No plaques will be forthcoming, only poems,
only the voices you hear in poems. Where are
the groans and sighs and bowls of cream? They're playing
other halls, when they can find them. It's harder
when liberal laws ensure the lawless places
are outlawed: so much for progress. Memory
hoists its flesh, its shambles, like a standard.

An Interview

'What did you see when they unrolled the bandage?'
'Everything was very grey and crumbly.
I did lift an arm, it was like a dead thing,
dropped right back; I thought that was terrible.
And the stench, to know it was your own, Jesus!'
'Speaking of whom, did he come back to see you?'
'Not he. He's like all shamans, do the job and
get the glory. He's off preaching somewhere.
Here am I with eyes like pits, limbs twitching,
clothes falling off me, sisters wailing, children
running from me in the street I'm so gruesome –
children I love, running away, you call this
living? What does he know about living?'
'Do you agree with those who wish to kill him?'
'Surely that is what he wants? We know them
these holy men, death-bringers even when they're
bringing the dead to life. They crucify the spirit.
He has destroyed a family for his greatness.'
'Some would say you really should be thankful.'
'Thankful for what? Look at me: a stick-insect.
Martha burnt the shroud. I scrubbed myself but
without purchase. I still smell those spices
that make the fetor worse. We are all dying
but is this to be borne, this death, this solitude?'
'Finally, have you a message for our readers?'
'Roll the stone right over me the next time.'

Urban Gunfire

'Civilians' are not really, truly, people.
As regimes fall, they're only 'caught in crossfire'.
Expendablest of the expendable, they
crawl, or if they're lucky someone drags them,
to doorways where they slump and shake till nightfall.
How great it must be not to be civilian
or anything but gun in hand, young, mobile,
slogan-fuelled better than machines are,
you cannot even hear the shattered housewife,
far less see her blood and bags and bread, it's
bullet time between you and your sniper,
hot streaks go shopping, nothing else goes shopping,
no one is out there in the open, we are,
we are it and it is where they vanish
like a clapped piece of tawdry human magic,
too feeble to be seen by psyched-up fighters.
Their cries are in another world. The trigger
is steady as they roll about the tarmac.
And it goes on as if it could not finish.

A Warning

What makes you think you have an acclamation?
Was it, they dragged the body of socialism
into a common grave, quicklime, dancing,
opening of cathedrals, minuet of
vestments as they cross the ancient incense,
ranks of dew-eyes dibbling trembling candles
in waxbound trays that never will grow freedom?
Musty but indefatigable reaction
stirs half-incredulously on one elbow
in another tomb as the bells clang, whistles,
laughs, clacks his grubby bones and orders suitings,
modest, subfusc, meeting the *novus ordo*
with decency. What, a republic a kingdom?
No no, there's nothing waiting in the wings, it's
early days. Take your string bag. An orange
will appear by magic, steaks, heroin, tickets
for strippers. Don't feel bought, you're buying, buying.
– And if, oh, if any should stint the euphoria
for a moment, watching the snow falling slowly
over shot-pocked facades, there'd only be some
muffled echo of the better life that
never seems to come, like a faint singing
heard in the pauses of snoring out of cardboard
or waiters' shouts from bursting blood-red kitchens.
They must listen so very hard, the freed ones!

A Night Sweat

I slept at last. It was a night of panthers.
In and out of something labyrinthine
which might have been bamboos, the smoky slinkers
appeared and disappeared, kept all their terror
tight, never looked to left or right, circled
finally (I knew they must) the tree I crouched in.
One head (that was enough) rocked, sniffed, swung upward,
flashed me a glare to melt tree-trunks, was part of
a mechanism that sketched more crawl than
spring up the bole and as if tentatively
clawed my overhanging leg and raked it
to tatters. What a shout it was I snatched it
back with, woke with, sweating, both hands clutching
the king of cramps, the furrowed spasm stretching
my very toes like claws, the panther's sinews
within me like a transplant, the pulsing ripples
of slowly untwisting muscles suddenly jerking
again and again, six, seven times, into searing
tautness as I tried to squirm the pain off
under the sheet or over the blanket (impossible, I know, you wait, you stick it).
There was a kind of morning in the offing,
an hour or so away. I was hardly breathing
as the last twitch subsided, had to dare to
move, exhausted into sweet relief that
turned me on the other side from panthers
(I hoped, and so it was). I slept to traffic
rolling by on its most ordinary business.

A Story

Once upon a time there was a story.
(Listen, children. Listen, wind. Listen, curtains.)
The story went to sea and stowed its oilskins.
It caught a fish farm and a cat-o-nine-tails,
a dog watch and some Mother Carey's chickens,
a donkey jacket and a weevil biscuit.
One night as it was swinging in its hammock,
tapping its darling tin of Golden Virginia
with one hand, while the other hand was trailing
down into the throbbing darknesses that
gathered to lick it, something quite gigantic
clamped itself to the keel and churned the vessel
round and down and round and down to drown there,
with hammocks catching fish, and fish tobacco.
The story had inflated its bright oilskins
and with a leap of most uncommon power
soared up and out over the waves, discharging
weak wet zigzag flashes in the moonlight.
Dawn found it shrinking, battered, leaky, falling,
dipping at last into the sea. The story
was now so small it hopped into a bottle
bobbing on a patch of phosphorescence.
On the Broomielaw I picked it up, and brought it
home (O curtains, O wind) and read its message
once upon a time (O children). How happy
it was it told me that homecoming ending.

Twilights

The darker darkness we have means to deal with,
it is the lighter darkness that confounds us,
the twilight of not knowing, the grey weighing,
the waiting, undisclosed and undisclosing,
the no day and the no night and the sickening
pause, the slow precipitate of phantoms.
Fog that fills the boat is worse than water.
I've seen some baling it hysterically
as if they could force out the imponderable –
they can't. Oh you must make a show of patience
even when patience is so hard to muster.
Soon you can see reluctant demons fading;
it must be something they can't stand; they're twisting
in their malevolent pain but they're transparent,
they're being entered, filled by something lighter,
they're being killed by what can only now be
sunlight, yes it's daybreak, the horizon
is like a seed-pod bursting to deliver
its one red melting fiery convex fruit-head,
loading the waves with those re-offered promises
of paths to take to brightness and best landfalls.
And such a loud wind fills the sails we're blustered
out of ourselves into a world of daylight,
of ropes, and spray, and clouds running and running.

A Skew

They proved the theory of surplus matter
by finding almost infinitely tiny
traces of the pipe the universe was
blown from, like a vase in Venice. Fragments
ranging through a dozen constellations
gave out at last a strangely twisted oval,
as if the blower had once been a jailbird,
blew as he spoke, with half his mouth. Onward,
the astronomers cried, fine, who needs a circle?
Better to live like flies in a bashed rummer
sweetened with fresh beer-dregs and froth-splotches
than skate a smiling perfect disc – incisive –
twice – three times – and drown. So they made merry
in orbit and on the mountain-tops, preparing
news of the skews, that was the phrase, for broadcast,
leaving the darker question of what prison
the gaunt primordial glassblower had starved in
before escaping to produce such matter
as he'd have wished a hundred times robuster
though not more perfect, if in imperfection
starriest anti-handedness prevailed there.

A Defence

I am told I should not love him, the magpie,
that he's a bully, but then I watch them bouncing
along the grass, chattering, black and white and
he and she, twigs in beak, the tree-top swaying
with half a nest in a hail-shower, the magpies
seeing off crows and gulls – a feint of mobbing
but who knows – eyeing a lost swan waddling
down the pavement, off course from Bingham's waters,
the smart bright bold bad pairing caring magpies
whose nest was blown down last December, back now
to build again, to breed again, to bring us
a batch of tumbling clockwork liquorice allsorts,
spruce, spliced, diced, learning to prance and hurtle
through evening and morning sycamores with what must be
something like happiness, the magpies, cocky,
hungry, handsome, an eye-catching flash for that
black and white collie to bark at, and the black and
white cat lurking under the car-bonnet
to lash a bushy tail at, and this page, seeing
these things, first white, now white and black, to pay its
tribute to, and lay out, thus, its pleasure.

A Sunset

Long rays take our long gaze out westward,
seaward, to the end of the city in waters,
almost dissolving thought in a drown of colours
where all definition would struggle to surface
from its puny swim of orange and crimson,
till something wrests us back, arrests the dreaming,
wrenches and clenches the body to face eastward:
the hospital's nine storeys are so fiery
it is a jolt to credit a reflection
with power to make one blank glass wall a blazing
cage for prisoner-patients to shout out from,
or so we'd think, with knotted sheets, their bedsteads
melting behind them, a jagged cry coming over –
but everything is calm, the brilliance fading
minute by minute into that absence
which is the ward only of imagination
uncurtains other pains and other panics
in real Gartnavel General, but leaving
a little warmth and sun, a little healing.

An Argument

'Whoever heard of a line ending *poem*?'
'You'd rather have the thud of *door-knob, jam-jar*?'
'Disgusting self-reflexiveness, I'd send it
packing.' 'I ask again, you want a *pick-axe*?'
'I want the line to get out and to stay out.'
'Walking through the universe one morning
I came across a cryptically clinging,
then tingling, singing tumbleweed, blown down there
as many ages as the wind had, fashioned
by sand as if it had been half hand-fashioned
and who knows if it was, the intricacies
were balled to figures like a sweated carving,
landscapes no less if you had eyes to mark them.
I held it light as a wish, would not have crushed it
for all the chisels, hammers, time-clocks, profits
it was not made from. I brought it through the desert –
you follow? – placed it here, not on this table
you're drumming at – why are you so impatient? –
but here, in line, where it becomes a poem.'
'What happened to the tumbleweed for chrissake?'
'I let it go of course; lovely; still tumbling.'

A Particular Country

No philosophers darkened that country.
Decreation, deconstruction died there
in the hot loamy burst of seedlings, squabs' teeth
cracking shells in zigzags, rain-forests
torn to shreds by squawks and shrieks that left them
untorn. As for general ideas,
a blowpipe picked them off, they joined the leaf-mould
to mulch minute minuter and minutest
particulars. Watered silk had nothing
on those vibrancies, creakings, thrustings, scatterings,
splash and flicker, drop and web, smudge and whirr, endless
intermitted unpredictable form-crinklings,
rhubarb-clumps with peacocks in a downpour,
what a sparkle of lushnesses, what a catmint
to roll in, what a maze of eyes to thread, that
mass of change and chance and challenge where you
go out; sink in; draw deep at signs that daze you
as stock might, in the nights of your own country.

A Coach-Tour (J.G.S.)

You did not know it, but nothing you could do to me
was worse than your silence when you were angry.
Often when I did wrong as a boy, my parents
refused the release of storming it out, pretended
I was not there, went on talking to each other,
brushing past me to wash and dry the dishes.
Nothing seemed more terrible, more cruel.
How can I say that, never nagged or beaten
as some are, or thrown out? We have to witness
what was, and those withdrawals, obliterations
planted such deadly fears of being abandoned
that when you made your face go blank and crossed your
legs and never let the jolting coach-tour
bring our bodies into faintest contact
I was cast back into an ancient panic,
sweating in my summer clothes, staring rigid
ahead, though gorgeous trees flashed past the window.
I saw a sole path that led out to ruins.
What did you feel? Ah but I know, exactly.

A Moratorium

Let us have no more memories, erase them.
Drive up to the moratorium doors where bouncers
are nailing archivists to hardwood panels.
You will not mention last year's drought, far less the
dinosaurs. 'Only a week ago, I –' 'Off with his
head.' 'Remember how you used to –' 'Off with
her head.' 'Once upon a time, children, there were –'
'Off with their heads.' The moratorium period
is one year, and in that year no past tenses
will be allowed. I want to see you all living –
and I mean living – you don't burnish the trumpet
you play the trumpet, you don't knot the quipu
you say this is the eighth of June the day of
sacrifices when we give the past its
obsidian. Runners on the altiplano
are up like jaguars. History's jugular
drips. A calendar snatched by a condor
flutters high and higher till the soaring
days dissolve in hungry sunlight. Gullets
of eternal blue – do you hear me – are terrifyingly,
gigantically, beautifully open.

A Fuchsia

I rescued it three years ago from rubbish.
Half-dead, a limp ungainly arc of ripped-off
green, it lay without a flower to recommend it
and somehow like a spring or snake it challenged
the logic of the vertical, resisted
potting; but I firmed it, staked it, waited.
Sometimes it's barish, sometimes bushy; tries, though.
This summer it decided to be bushy,
parachutes pushed out, dangling pink and purple,
trembling as container lorries rumbled,
almost nodding to make me say I loved them,
and so I do, you hear that, you strange plant you,
it's true. You don't love me but I sense something –
no I can't be mistaken, it's next to palpable –
you're bent, a down-turned cup-hook, and without propping
you would collapse into the earth you came from,
so why should you keep flowering so gamely –
I can't but think it speaks to me, your living
loaded curve of grace steadily bearing,
but the best bearing, the best blooming, is moral,
or if that cannot be – who am I to say so,
is chlorophyll so dumb – at least I'm sending,
like an antenna – don't shake, I don't mean insects –
waves of encouragement, solidarities of
struggle, gratitude even for imaginary
gratitude, though who knows what a fuchsia
feels, plucked from dump and dust, from a gehenna
to this west kitchen window, rays of evening
and more mysterious light of human glances.

The Last Intifada

It seems a sunny window morning murmur
with arms on sills. You sense the trembling house-plants
as planes roar past below the radar, bringing
safety and terror. Non-existent trumpets
are heard to take the lid off some repair-shop.
You speak, everyone speaks, the dusty city
is like a bush of sparrows. The streets are filling,
and now what might be nearhand seas – it's not though –
are breaking, crashing, seething back, and breaking.
Where is the throne? Where are the iron gods then,
with their gold racks and fiery chairs, tormentors
and cowardly commanders, is it bunkers,
morions, pretorians, doors dead to keypads?
Blisters travel on their grounded gunships.
What are the iron gates once they are broken?
Whose is the throne that makes a little firewood?
What happened to the gods that found a million –
oh no, not money, but a million people –
swarming over their guards and gravely singing,
sternly singing but with grave exultation,
stern assurance, a strange forward movement
that cut a swathe like a sea surge, the voices
rising and falling and the high sun shining?
They're dying. They are dying, they are dying.

A Flypast

Symphonic shreds had just swept off with Schnittke
when two swans flew like spirits past my window.
Russia, music, soul, said the television,
nature, it said, harmony, ideal.
The long necks stretched, smelt their swan lake, laboured
forward till the trees hid them. And eastern,
the television said, Armenian, Azeri
horizontality, the patterns endless,
keeping western verticals at bay while
voices circle over silent marshes.
Well, I don't know. My startling flyers flapping
so steady and so low over the van-tops,
the hissing wheels, the sirens and the skateboards,
knew where they were going and had shattered
in their rising from some placid water mirror
a harmony too famous, strode the air-streams
to turn how many heads at windows as we
wonder that we ever thought them spirits,
those muscles working, those webs, that eye, that purpose.

A Black Dog Day

Pour, pour down, light like water, any acre,
any square or warren, any crossroads
of this habble will do. Drench them with your searches,
flash-flood the sweating truncheons from their dust-clouds,
fall pitilessly on the tear-gassed babies,
wash us with our lies into the syvers.

Tram-Ride, 1939 (F.M.)

How cold it is to stand on the street corner
at nineteen, in the foggy Glasgow winter,
with pinched white face and hands in pockets, straining
to catch that single stocky gallus figure
who might be anyone but was one only;
prowling a few feet – not too far! – glanced at
idly by the patient Cosmo queue, growing
exposed, your watch burning, how long now, yes but,
what, half an hour, some eyes saying, Stood up, eh? –
until the step has to be taken, casually,
you have to stroll off, what's won by staying?
he won't appear (he had simply forgotten,
you didn't know that then), and on the top deck
of a southbound tram you stare into the window
as it reflects a mask about to shake with
ridiculous but uncontrollable tears, a choking
you gulp back instantly, no one has heard it,
shameful – shameful – to be dominated
by such emotions as the busy tramful
of half indifferent, half curious folk would
mock at if they knew, and would they sometime,
in half a century perhaps, accept that love is
what it is, that tears are what they are, that
Jack can shiver in the numbing close-mouth
of missing dates for Jill or Jake, and suffer?

A Water Horse

Impossibly a totality of water
dragonlike some force must surely have uttered
creature from underground chaos emerging
shook itself loose of almost clovelike grits and
grouts and with such thrustful bunched mounting
of air as made a bellying of night-clouds
rose glittering and bucketing over mountains
till at last the moon the unconscionable rider
tugged its unbridled hide and slowly cantered
across the universe, a shine upon a
shine, a whinny from a throat of water.

Whistling

These coal-black horses were not made of water.
Their half-stripped ramrod riders more like androids
than mercenaries bounced in their stirrups, swearing
from mouths like slits, giving invisible nudges
to iron flanks that knew their masters. The horses
clattered across the courtyard for an airing,
heartily slapped by stable-boys, snorting
and farting between snorts, a morning freedom
before kettledrums. Not a beat yet, only skylarks
rising from the long grass all round, and rustlings
half-sensed where the wind picked a grove. The riders
might have eaten larks, but never heard them,
or if they did it entered generally
into a wellbeing they need never examine,
keeping a tight rein with blank mind, but whistling
suddenly, tunelessly through their teeth, almost
interminably at last, hardly more meaningfully
than the field river not far off, rehearsing
what it could not say better, over and over,
yet we might lean to thinking them more human.
Fugitives heard that whistling, froze, and shivered.

A Sling

A figure came slowly out of the forest
with a child. She was in rags and had been crying
but that was over. Her glance was like steel to
those watching. The boy in his blue coat gathered
her wrist where it had been hanging loosely, not for
protection or out of fear but as if her body
was not his mother but a graven weapon
he would sling willing hard inexplicable
against the perpetrators, the oppressors.
He would say nothing, but he would see them crying.
Their cursed horses curvet, clash their stirrups.

The Last Scoria

It was well beyond the visible, that furnace.
Nothing lurid played on the assayers.
They sat in white coats at their winking switchboards.
Millions of dead souls crackled in the bonfire
unheard, with unimaginable refinement
breaking down, down, breaking down, breaking
into what delicatest robot tongs would
quietly withdraw from the roaring, something like
loaves as of platinum, set on trays, cooling,
ready to sustain what? whole heavens of
angels, hells of demons? – burn their fingers,
watch it, all the human pain can never
quite be taken out, tongues even of spirits
will sting on the indignant smelt. Controllers
press their final indifferent keys, the raking
begins, of empires, schools of thought, oppressions,
censors, treacheries, secret executions,
stonings, unknown soldiers, vivisections,
the starved, the slag, the sum of that, the scoria.

Sunday in East Mars

Poems come from East Mars, said Spicer,
and so they do. Our most perjink transmitters,
miniaturized to the last murmur, for protection
against not only probes but all explorers,
push out particles of that strenuous pleasure
you do your best to record. Intermittent
the bursts are, not to be taken for granted.
We want you not to know, and not to manage.
We think you manage far too much. We'd never
send you a scenario, a storyboard, a legend,
but we do and in our own time endlessly will
give you signals that show greater power's
in stories than in story. What is adjustment?
Giving up. What is a whole? A sum of
parts done wrong. Oh if outgrowing of concepts –
we tap our keys with some fervour here – is dolphins
that slice the air into dripping arcs, figureheads
brighter than any boat was ever fixed to,
we think we've seen inexplicable helpers
that might sustain a castaway. Delight is
use and use delight, and when you write you
move the shape of things that millimetre
it needs to breathe, be reassured of living,
not that it ever was not living, but flickers
and shiftings of its great mass are so sanative
it grows, re-forms yet never forms, advances
in its own dimensions.   It is like a Sunday
here. We are very calm. Scarlet nasturtiums
twine with vigorous will between the boulders.
I love to watch them when I'm not transmitting.
We'd send you one, but then you have it, don't you?

An Atrium

At first we loved the plate-glass glare, the car-horns,
the swarthy shoppers and the garrulous market –
I haggled a set of skewers for 'what kebabs would
that be?' you said laughing – but we sauntered
out of the heat at last, through a huge doorway,
into a hall made cool with many fountains,
green with high palms like columns, silver-columned
with steel like stylized palms, a floor of marble,
and faint muzak from unseen grilles drifting
among the water-drops to make real music,
Cage-like, as our shoes clacked in. Above us –
we could hardly not look up – seemed endless –
the vast round space retreated to the plainest
of pure blue domes that only its gentle shining
showed as not the sky we thought we wanted.
We were enclosed in a great peace pretending
to infinity; the infinity of thinking
came to us without pretence, with wonder, gladness,
amazed fall of the shell of self to the marble,
diamond awareness of others like coloured jewels
walking, talking, smoking, smiling slowly
or sitting on stone benches with their papers,
watching their children dip a hand in waters
that had left paradise that very midday
and brought it to them, brought it to them. Surely
we too were moved by gifts we'd never chaffered,
the poor brass toys we clutched had become earnests
of something we would never define, not golden,
not silver, not even green, but only
a murmur, a goodness, a gushing spring, an echo.

A Full Moon

The moon with its old beauty and blank power,
crisscrossed by unseen unchanging bootprints –
take a curler's broom to sweep your tracks back! –
slinks from left to right above the roof-tops –
I'm watching it, that's my reluctant tribute
to a mass of rock with light on its deserts –
and vanishes steadily beyond a sight-line
that suddenly seems deprived, left in a blankness
greater than the moon's – crane, strain, the house-wall's
got it, someone else's window's filling,
it's all right! – but the mind, magnetized, misses
the dark man gathering sticks in the story,
the rayed craters of reality, the voyage
of an image soldered into imagination
by the megalith builders and those before them,
and if there were giants on the earth, well then,
they would make their bonfires by its brilliance
and shout at it, wading their stormy foreshore.
I rise and switch the light off like a lift-off.

Golden Apples

Bradbury, we all want to go to the sun, man!
It's in our veins, we want to scoop it cleanly –
everything that seems impossible, we want it –
to tangle with those lavish prominences,
to eat that heat, to get a golden gauntlet,
to lay our heart at the very heart of the matter.
What a bath of neutrinos, would that not cleanse us?
And helium wings to shoot us through the static?
They say it's all gas, but is that really likely?
We have to find some way to fix our footsteps
like plaques of blacker fire in fire. We have to
be there, to have been there, to return if
sometime we should need to. What is freedom –
couch potatoes at the end of the millennium,
a bingo card, a pub harangue, *Neighbours*?
The craft must stand a million degrees, roughly.
Roughly stand, or roughly a million? Both, with
no guarantee! This is not science fiction.
Lateral thinking scrubs refrigeration
as the only hope. Phoenix and salamander
hint heat is conquered by habitatizing,
not fending off. What fish wear macintoshes?
I can see navigators burning like poets,
boiling like Picts without a stitch of armour,
bolts from the blue that run into the unblue,
themselves both it and not it, gold and ungold,
not melted by but melting, staring, into
groves of energy, billets of resurgence.
And where else should they be, our navigators?

Fires

What is that place, my father and my mother,
you have gone to, I think of, in the ashes
of the air and not the earth, better to go there
than under stones or in any remembrance
but mine and that of others who once loved you,
fewer year on year. It is midsummer
and till my voice broke, *Summer suns are glowing*
I loved to sing and *One fine day* to hear from
some thin wild old gramophone that carried
its passion across the Rutherglen street, invisibly
played again and again – I thought of that person,
him or her, as taking me to a country
far high sunny where I knew to be happy
was only a moment, a puttering flame in the fireplace
but burning all the misery to cinders
if it could, a sift of dross like what we mourn for
as caskets sink with horrifying blandness
into a roar, into smoke, into light, into almost nothing.
The not quite nothing I praise it and I write it.

A Pedlar

An old man selling joy comes round here sometimes.
His case weighs down, no one seems to want it.
Buttonless coat and battered cardboard stand there
like diffidence made monumental. Promise –
of anything – never seemed further, blanker.
Who would not slam a door on such a scarecrow?
If any lingered, his entire persuasion
was to look at them, hangdog, hand on case-lock,
waiting to be asked to unroll treasures.
Not that way, never that way, hopeless person!
Even his trudging back was not reproachful.
– But anyway there came a day, today, be honest,
when if something changeable bluff bright cloudy
in the air and such a brash sun shouldering branches
recharged his speech I can only imagine –
but he flung open the case and suddenly was saying
'What is not there is hardly worth desiring,
do you not agree? Is it not fine? Others
have said so, whenever I could elicit
a bit of truth from pursed lips. Pursed and zipped is
what I mean! You tell them it's quite costly
they vanish behind their mortises. Pedlars?
No thanks. Yet four wheels to the hypermarket –
get boys to load your boot with wine and salmon –
a shark steak for a laugh, some avocados –
perhaps a large pavlova if *they're* coming –
will not purr back with it, don't be deluded,
since only what you do not want to pay for
is what I have: I do not sell for money.
But if you can lay out a little pain, it's business.
Break a pig of disappointments, frustrations.
An old billfold of hopes deferred? Only
if it aches, aches. Look at what I have here,
this, and these. The price is not beyond you?
'No no,' I said, 'no, it's not, no, I'll have some.'

An Iraqi Student

Quiet spoken Sabbar Sultan in Basra,
I hope you are well as I am unwarlike.
Belligerent Americans are baking
in Arabia, itching to terrify your cities.
May they not, nor you theirs. But shall we ever
resume new-old conclusions about Titus,
Gormenghast, the great flood, Fuchsia, Steerpike?
The walls are higher now, the roads a minefield.
It would be very bad to be forgetful.
One thin line of thought in words, not shifting
as sands are – well, not quite so shifting, language
shifts with anchors dragging – must manage
like a camel-train to make its measured progress
through missile banks, camouflage fatigues, gas-masks
clustered like decapitated insects –
future ruins already lightly dusted
by the desert wind. I hope you tell your students
of this wet green periphery, of reading
Durrell and Bunting, Murdoch and MacDiarmid,
under Gothic – well, not really Gothic – arches;
add commandeered Strathclyde, as missile-haunted
as now the Gulf is, 'The Bunkers of Glen Fruin'
an unwritten skirl, but anyone can hear it.
Keep safe; the edge is everywhere; all know it.

A Lintel

Nobody knows how many times the city
has been rebuilt. People like to live there.
Ten millenniums of impacted boneyards
offer no counter-thrust to the piledrivers
as white-veranda'd skyscrapers, unblasted
yet, rise and flaunt what ancient board-games,
half-understood among the skulls, might bet on,
so well-thumbed is the book of revolutions.
'Would not we shatter it to bits' – or try to,
and find the world is a high-fired clay letter
fused to its hard clay envelope. We break it –
yes yes, of course we do – and lose the message.
The oven roars again, communicating
another time, a later wisdom, templates
of penthouses that will become their own cellars,
home for lobbed grenades and searchlights. We live here!
The sniped-at or the earthquake-dizzy concrete
cracks. No one swears we won't go back there!
Even if it should be bare hands time, the jackals
can roam elsewhere, you have a tent you have a
tower. Time-capsules? Those are for children.
We live and die miles down miles up in faience
and porphyry and oil and steel and denim,
saluting them – what, the ages? – as they melt out,
I don't say what they are, melt out delivering
their more than half misunderstood but fiery
cut of wedges tight across our lintel.

A Manifesto

The futurists took ties to yellow parties.
The futurists thought life a bobby-dazzler.
The futurists made heady love to airships.
The futurists made heavy words go heady.
The futurists got canvas off its hindlegs.
The futurists threw music off its shirtfront.
The futurists gesamtkunstwerked the bolshies.
The futurists shot off montage's visa.
The futurists flew kites up up up endless.
The futurists kept dynamos in kennels.
The futurists had soaring paper cities.
The futurists lie snoring in real cities.
The futurists are dreaming of red pigeons.
The futurists hold hands among the atoms.
The futurists, united, shall never be defeated.
The futurists, united, shall never be defeated.
The futurists, united, shall never be defeated.

A Leavetaking

It faded down the valley, out of earshot.
The backs were straight, the music was so jaunty
they must have dwindled braced by sightless wishes.
They wave them off and then they stand there watching,
the wives and daughters, the lovers, the three sisters.
Slowly they turn, when they can expect nothing
to be seen or heard except the dry burning valley
with startling broom-pods bursting to remind them
of life and its undeviating purpose.
They are a part of what it is as daily
and not in crises they are walking, working,
one of them pausing to straighten a small picture
and be left staring into it unseeing
as if it framed another world, a better,
although she knows there's none, and that is better.

A Crow

The summer grows late, cool, ragged, precious.
Clouds like ungainly brooms are sweeping showers
across the slates. On a dripping lamp-standard
a crow hunches, flaps, hunches. The young painter
with his tin of white sings as he hops in and
out of the rain. The sun bursts what it has been saving
so suddenly, so brilliantly, we are smiling.
It is August still. The leaves hang fast and glisten.
If there were no seasons, who would be singing?
If there was no weather, who would be painting?
If there was no earth turning, we darkly, partly
think, no crow would have a lawn to stamp on,
or Aristarchus any globe to dandle.
As not to be born is worst – a crow will tell you,
a worm will tell you – not to be created
crosses galaxies like a shadow of horror.
But created they are; born, I and the painter;
really wet ruffled shiny black half-happy
the feathers of the raucous-hearted clatterer.

Lamps

And if anyone should tell our adventures,
remember that the universe has spaces
as well as forms – abysses, deserts, niches,
distances without even time as pedlar
to bring you, if you waited, explanations.
No, we have seen what we have seen, but often
there is a blank you must not fill with monsters.
It is all for what is to come after.
It is for the duguth of firm intent, the voyage
he and she and they must take, and you quiet
but trembling in your chair, rising, following
the light you catch, swinging but never vanishing,
into great deeps, our helmet-lamps, beckoning.

Translations

CLAUDIAN

On the Old Man of Verona: A Deconstruction

Auld Fergus is richt bien an croose, ye ken,
Crawin on his ain dunghill seeventy years.
His stick hirples him ower the grun he crowled on
Langsyne. Gode, he wis feart tae lea the hoose!
His teeth ay chittert at the notion o chynge.
Aw furrin lochs were pysin! That export trock –
Nae thanks! The ermy? – na, thon's danger-money.
Boather the ombudsman? Naw, keep the heid doon.
He's sic a sumph he's niver been tae toon,
He gawks up at the lift – weel, it's free, man!
He coonts the months by kail and coarn and claver,
But disna ken his M.P. frae his elbuck.
Same auld fields, same sun an muin – aw's wan
Tae him, he plowters through, it's breid an bu'er.
He kent that aik as an aikorn wance? – big deal!
The scrunty foggage is as grey as him.
And Bennachie's as faur aff as Benares,
And as for Udny, oh man, yon's like Omsk.
Warst thing is, he's still quite hale an stuffie,
His sons and oys are hodden doon, pair loons.
Their backpacks are stashed fidgin for Albania:
He's gote his wee warld, but they wahnt the Wey.

['De sene Veronensi']

Bien comfortable   croose self-satisfied   hirples limps   grun ground
lea leave   trock business   sumph fool   lift sky   kail cabbage
claver clover   elbuck elbow   wan one   plowters works sloppily
foggage grass, grazing   stuffie sturdy   oys grandsons
hodden doon held back   pair loons poor fellows   fidgin itching

MICHELANGELO BUONARROTI

'In me is daith . . .'

In me is daith, I leeve in you alane.
Ye twin time aff and mark it, gie oot time
tae gar me loup or shauchle as ye will.

Leeze me on your mense! For I can sain
the saul that's no run through by bornheid time:
ye mak it staun and luk at Gode, stock-still.

['In me la morte . . .']

Leeve live   *twin* split   *gar* make   *loup* leap   *shauchle* shamble
leeze me on I am happy with   *mense* grace   *sain* bless   *bornheid* headlong
staun stand

GIACOMO LEOPARDI

The Aesome Blackie

Therr ye sit, at the tap o the auld tour,
aesome blackie, giein the kintraside your sang
afore the cowslem taks wir licht awaw;
the haill glen swaws wi thae sweet rins o soun.
Aw roon, spring's bricht and braw
in ilka airt, and fields expreme their joy;
whase hert sees this, melts richt aipen and nesh.
Herk tae the baain sheep, the rowtin o the kye!
The ither happy burdies wheel thegither
in rival bauns, the braid lift taks their flisks
and flirts in thoosans, it's their hoaliday!
But you sit aye apairt, thochtfu; nae whisks
alang the airs for you,
nae croods o friens; nae licht-hertit gemms;
yit your sang shemms
the best flooer o your life and o this May.

Wae's me tae see hoo near
your weys tae mine! Pleesure and lauchtir that gar
the halflin mind pit oan its pleyin-gear,
love that is youdith's furst confiderat
and the sherpest-taen sich o aulder years –
I've nae likin for thae, I kenna why;
seem tae flee them, faur aff,
like a gangrel body, a nyaff
tae his ain fowk, a traiveller
through his ain unhanty livin spring.
This day, which noo dwines doon tae the gloamin,
is taen here as a people's hoaliday.

Aesome solitary   *blackie* blackbird   *cowslem* evening   *wir* our
swaws ripples   *rins o soun* streams of sound   *in ilka airt* everywhere
aipen open   *nesh* tender   *rowtin* lowing   *kye* cattle   *bauns* bands
lift sky   *gemms* games   *gar* make   *halflin* young   *sich* sigh
thae those   *gangrel body* wanderer   *nyaff* despised person
unhanty clumsy

Herk hoo the bells jow oot through the lown air,
and hoo the shoatguns aften crack their thunner
fae faur-aff villa tae villa reverbin awwhere.
Aw in their hoaliday claes,
the boays and lassies skail
fae their hooses and stravaig fae street tae street;
the gled hert and the wandrin ee are theirs!
Burdalane, I gaze
alang thae unthrang fields, gang my ain gate,
pit aff tae ither times aw gemms and ploys;
my een threid the douce air
and stap at the sun abune his faur hill-taps
steekin this lang lown day:
he draps and's gane, and whit he says by this
is, even gleddest youthheid canna stay.

You, solitar burdie, wance ye come
tae the eenin o the span your weird decreets,
I'm shair ye'll no decry
the life ye've leeved; the things ye thocht maist fain
were nature's alane.
But me, gin the years hain
me intae hatit auldness,
and thir een canna speak tae ithers' herts,
and aw the warld be tim, and my days tae come
mair seik and bleck nor aw the days that's gane,
my wiss tae be alane,
hoo will it seem? and hoo thae years? and me?
A cutty-stool I see,
and mony backwart luik and unappeasit grane.

['Il passero solitario']

<hr>

jow toll   lown calm   skail scatter   burdalane quite alone   steekin closing
gin if   hain protect   thir these   tim empty
cutty-stool stool of repentance   grane groan

GIACOMO LEOPARDI

Flinder

ALICK

I tell ye, Malc, thon wes an eerie widdrim
I hud yestreen, it aw comes back tae mind
noo I see the muin again. I wes staunin
at the winnock that luiks richt ower the fields;
I kest my een up tae the lift, and wow
but the muin cam loose, in a gliff: I thocht
it tumml't doon, the muckle thing, cam near
and near, till it hud whumml't wi a scult
amang the stooks, breenged therr aboot the size
o a creel, and scowdert oot a michty boak,
a clood o flichters that soon hisht and pisht
like coaly gleeds a haun hes smoort ablow
the watter-troch. I sweer there wes nae differ:
richt in the middle o the field it wes,
the muin, and oot it gaed, gaed slawly bleck;
the gress aw roon began tae sneyster and smeek.
I luikit up again intae the lift:
naethin wes left bar a skimmer, a smick, a neuk
it hud been claucht fae, and yon wes a sicht
that gart my bluid rin cauld: I'm shakkin yit.

MALC

As weel ye micht. It's aiblins on the cairds
the muin could traipse doon someday tae yir rigs.

Flinder fragment   *widdrim* nightmare   *yestreen* last night
winnock window   *lift* sky   *gliff* moment   *whumml't* tumbled
scult slap   *breenged* barged   *scowdert* scorched   *boak* vomit
flichters particles   *gleeds* embers   *smoort* smothered   *ablow* below
sneyster burn   *smeek* smoke   *skimmer* gleam   *smick* spot
claucht clutched   *gart* made

ALICK

Wha kens? Is it no true hoo simmer gies us
shuitin-starns?

MALC

                    Ay, but there's starns eneuch:
it's little skaith gif yin or twa sud faw –
there's thoosans mair. But we've allanerly
the aesome muin i the lift, and naebody
hes watched it faw, binna in dwam or widdrim...

[Frammento: 'Odi, Melisso...']

---

skaith damage   *allanerly* only   *aesome* solitary   *binna* unless
dwam daydream

GIACOMO LEOPARDI

Tae his sel

Noo and for aye, ye'se be quate,
my forfochen hert. Gane is the graun swick
I thocht wad be ayebydin. Gane. I'm shair
yon swick, though sweet, is ower:
I hope for't and I streetch for't noo nae mair.
Quate, for aye. Eneuch
o that yaiseless pit-pat. Naethin is wurth
your eident flutherins, ye can sich and sab
tae a yirth that's deif. Whit's life
but a wide wersh wanrufe; the warld's but a clart.
Quate, quate. It is
the last wanhope. For there is nae weird gien
tae livin men bar daith. Wha'd no miscaw
you, nature, grim   •
in your slee and ugsome pooer tae ding us doon,
and aathing circumjackless, howe, and tim.

['A se stesso']

Quate at peace   forfochen worn-out   swick deception   eident eager
sab sob   wersh tasteless, insipid   wanrufe disquiet, restlessness
clart lump of filth   wanhope despair   weird fate   slee sly   ding throw
circumjackless uncircumscribed   howe hollow   tim empty

101

ALEKSANDR PUSHKIN

Autumn (A Fragment)

Then, what is not the target for my drowsy mind?
Derzhavin

1

October has come – already now the wood
Casts its last leaves, its branches are all bare;
Autumn has breathed its cold to freeze the road,
Beyond the mill the stream still murmurs there,
But the pond's already ice; my neighbour's load
Of hunting-hounds is shot off with wild blare
To ravage winter crops in distant fields;
They bay until the sleeping forest yields.

2

Now is my time: I hold no brief for spring;
Tiresome thaw with its slush and stench – I'm ill
In spring, blood fevered, mind and heart panting
With longing. Rough-hewn winter meets the bill
Far better; I love its snows; our sledge stealing
Through moonlight, swift, at its own airy will,
While a warm hand stirs from beneath her sable
To press my hand, and make her flush and tremble!

3

What a delight to glide on sharp-shod iron
Across the smooth unruffled river-glass!
Winter festivals all shimmer and fire!...
But snow for six months? No, I think I'll pass:
Even for bears in dens it might be fine
At first, but not at last. You can't amass
Pleasure for ever from Juliet in a sledge,
Or vegetate by stove and window-ledge.

4

Summer, you beauty! I would be truly yours
But for the heat and dust, the midges and the flies.
You drain our mental strength, and what tortures
You give us! Like the field, the body cries
For rain; to be where drink and freshness pours;
Only to see old mother winter rise
Once more: pancakes and wine for her farewell,
Ice and ice-cream for her memorial.

5

Late autumn days are no one's favourite,
And yet, you know, I find this season dear.
Its still beauty, its shining placid spirit
Attract me like a Cinderella's tear.
I tell you frankly I can see no merit
In any other season of the year.
Such good, in autumn? Yes, I can discover
Its beckoning essence, and I am no boastful lover.

6

How to persuade you? Were you ever taken
By some unrobust girl wasting away –
Strange, but it's like that. She is stricken,
Death-bent, poor creature, unrepining prey
Of unseen jaws whose grip will never slacken;
She smiles still, with red lips that fade to grey;
Her face has twilight in its blood, not dawn;
Alive today, tomorrow she is gone.

7

Melancholy time, yet magic to the sight!
Leavetaking kinds of beauty please me best:
All nature withering in a sumptuous light,
The groves and forests gold-and-purple-dressed,
The wind-loud tree-crests, the airy delight,
The mists that roll to trouble the sky's rest,
The rare sun-ray and the first test of frost,
The distant menace of winter's grizzled ghost.

8

And with each autumn I bud and bloom once more;
The Russian cold is good and therapeutic;
The everyday routines no longer bore:
Hunger and sleep come sweetly automatic;
Joy dances lightly where my heart's tides pour,
Desire swirls up – I'm young again, an addict
Of life and happiness – that's my organism
(And please forgive this forced prosaicism).

9

My horse is brought; it shakes its mane and takes
Its rider out into the wilderness,
The frostbound glen where every hoofbeat strikes
Flashes, rings loud, while ice cracks in the stress.
But the short day goes grey, and the fire-flakes
Play up in the forgotten grate, now less,
Now more, now smouldering and now flaring:
I read there, or I feed my long thoughts, staring.

10

And I forget the world – and in dear silence
Am dearly lulled by my imagination,
And poetry wakens into consciousness:
My soul is rocked in lyric agitation,
It cries and trembles, and like a dreamer frets
To free itself in full manifestation –
And now a swarm of unseen guests draws near,
Both old friends and imagined shapes are here.

11

And brave thoughts break like waves along my brain,
And rhymes race forward to the rendezvous,
And pen beckons to finger, paper to pen.
One minute, and verse surges freely through.
So a stilled ship drowses on the stilled main,
Till look: a sudden leaping of the crew,
Masts are shinned up and down, sails belly free,
The huge mass moves and slices through the sea.

12

Great to sail off with it! But where to go?
What lands shall we now see: vast Caucasus,
Or some sun-blistered Moldavian meadow,
Or Normandy's snow-gleaming policies,
Or Switzers' pyramid array on show,
Or wild and sad Scottish rock-fortresses...?

['Osen'']

. . . . . .

Corbie tae corbie flees and steirs,
Corbie tae corbie skreiks and speirs:
Corbie! whaur sall we tak meat?
And hoo kin we fin oot aboo't?

Corbie tae corbie gies repone:
Ah ken the brod oor denner's oan;
In aipen muir, unner a sauch,
A knicht liggs thonner, deid eneuch.

Whae kill't thoan boay, and forwhy,
His faucon kens that anerly,
And his mear sae corbie-bleck,
And his ying wife, tae this effeck:

The faucon's flittit tae the shaw,
The reiver's rid the mear awaw,
But the wife's aye waukin fur
Nae deid man but her leevin dear.

['Voron k voronu letit...' Pushkin's untitled Russian version of
the old Scottish ballad 'The Twa Corbies'.]

Corbie raven   *steirs* stirs, sets out   *speirs* asks   *repone* reply   *brod* table
aipen open   *sauch* willow   *anerly* alone   *mear* mare   *reiver* raider
waukin wakeful, watching

VLADIMIR SOLOVYOV

The Wintry Loch o Saimaa

Happit in a flaffie mantie fae heid tae feet
Ye ligg like a stookie in a dwam, white, quaet.
The leamin skimmerin snawy air micht hint,
But disnae by the sleeest souch, o daith.

Naw naw, I hivnae socht ye yaiselesslie
In aw thon boddomless lown doverin.
Faur ben, my sicht is on nae blawflum o ye,
Nikniven! – queen o pine and craig and whin!

Mackless as the snaw ayont the braes,
Thocht-hoatchin like the daurkest yuletide nicht,
Ye blinter wi the Merry-Dancers' bleeze,
Dochter o sooty Chaos, eerie-bricht!

['Na Saime zimoi']

Happit wrapped   *mantie* gown   *stookie* statue   *dwam* daydream
quaet quiet   *leamin gleaming*   *souch* breath   *lown* calm, hushed
doverin dozing   *ben* within   *blawflum* deluding image
Nikniven medieval witch queen   *mackless* immaculate
thocht-hoatchin rich with many thoughts   *blinter* shimmer

ALEKSANDR BLOK

. . . .

Nicht, causey, leerie, pothicar,
Aw'where a dreich and donnert licht.
Leeve for twinty-five year mair –
Naethin will chynge. Nane taks flicht.

Ay, ye can dee – re-stert it aw,
Aw'thing turns roon like a peerie:
Nicht, and the canaul's cauld swaw,
Causey, pothicar, and leerie.

['Noch', ulitsa...']

Causey street   *leerie* lamp   *dreich* bleak   *donnert* dull   *peerie* top

VELIMIR KHLEBNIKOV

Gaffin-Cantrip

Och, unsneck, snicherers!
Och, unsnib, snicherers!
Gar thaim smicker wi smirlin, gar thaim smirkle skirlinlie,
Och, snicher smirtlinlie!
Och, the snorkstock o the besnorkit – the smue o the besmuit
    snicherers!
Och, snocher snowkilie, smirl o the snirkit snirters!
Snowkio, snorkio,
Smirl and snitter, sneeterers and sneisterers,
Snicherikins and snocherikins.
Och, unsneck, snicherers!
Och, unsnib, snicherers!

['Zaklyatie smekhom']

Gaffin-cantrip incantation by laughter   *gar* make
The original is a sound-poem built up on imaginative extensions of the word *smekh*
(laughter). Scots equivalents are similarly deployed here.

VELIMIR KHLEBNIKOV

Ha-oo!

Ha-oo! ha-oo! ha-oo!
Many of the black ones
Ha-oo! ha-oo! ha-oo!
Dogs of the rebellion
Ha-oo! ha-oo! ha-oo!
Scampered through the snow
Ha-oo! ha-oo! ha-oo!
To the nearby villages
Ha-oo! ha-oo! ha-oo!
To root up all the corpses
Ha-oo! ha-oo! ha-oo!
To drag off someone's arm
Ha-oo! ha-oo! ha-oo!
To bloody up their muzzles
In belly and in snow.

['Gau! gau! gau!']

VELIMIR KHLEBNIKOV

Coarse Talk

COARSE TALK
Here's a kick in the teeth –
My kiss.
More red,
More scarlet,
A coarse rowan,
A fragged-out fragging,
A red cart-shaft,
Cherry-blossoms,
Crushed-up lips.
And the air screaming.

['Gruby yazyk']

111

VLADIMIR MAYAKOVSKY

For All That

The street's caved in like a syphilitic's nose.
The river's a libidinous ripple of spittle.
The park, in tiniest wisp of underclothes,
lies sprawled with its midsummer titill-

ation. I walked into the square,
pulled a burnt-out neighbourhood
over my head like a ginger hairpiece.
People are scared – foot by foot
a half-chewed shout crawls from my face.

But they won't bark at me, they won't condemn me,
they'll strew my prophet's path with flowers.
None of the caved-in noses will blame me:
I am your poet, I am yours.

Your terrible judgement is as terrifying as a teashop!
Prostitutes will hoist me alone like a monstrance
through the burning tenements, their gestures teaching
God to absolve and not to admonish.

And God will start crying over my slim volume! –
not words but spasms, lumps clamped together;
and he'll run through heaven with my poems under his arm
and read them out, panting, to those in his favour.

['A vse-taki']

EUGENIO MONTALE

Boats on the Marne

Elegant delight of the cork-float
caught in the current that
wavers through inverted bridges
and the full moon pale in the sun:
boats on the river, frisky, summer-borne,
and a dull murmur from the city.
Row by the meadow, if the butterfly-hunter
should reach you with his net,
the tree-maze on the wall where dragon's
blood is re-done in red ochre.

Voices on the river, bursts of sound from the banks,
or rhythmic dip and rise of canoes
in the evening that ripples
through the manes of the walnut-trees, but where is
the steady procession of the seasons
that was a dawn without streets and without end,
where is the long wait and what is the emptiness
that leaves us nothing to defend?

This is the dream: an enormous
unending day flooding and reflooding
its almost unwinking glare between the dykes,
and the good work of man at every turn,
a veiled tomorrow carrying no terror.
And the dream was other things, but its reflection,
strong on the racing water, under the hanging
tit's nest, airy and inaccessible,
was supreme silence in the concerted
cry of midday and the evening
was a longer morning, the great ferment
a great rest.
             Here . . . the enduring colour
is that of the mouse jack-in-the-box
among the reeds or the starling with its spurt
of poisonous metal swallowed up
by the misty bank.

Here is the dusk. We now
can go down till the Great Bear shows its face.

(Sunday boats on the Marne, a race
on the day of your anniversary.)

['Barche sulla Marna']

EUGENIO MONTALE

Wind in the Crescent (Edinburgh)

The muckle brig didna gang your wey.
Gid ye'd've gien the word, I'd have won through
to ye by navigatin stanks and syvers. But
aa my virr, wi thon sun on the winnocks
o the verandas, wis seepin slawly awa.

A birkie that wis preachin on the Crescent
speirit at me: 'D'ye ken whaur Gode is?' I kent
and tellt him. He shook his heid. I saw nae mair
o him in the wud wind that skelpit hooses and fowk
and gart them flee abune the taurry daurk.

['Vento sulla mezzaluna']

Gin if   *stanks* gutters   *syvers* drain-traps   *virr* vitality
winnicks windows   *birkie* chap   *speirit* asked   *wud* mad   *gart* made

115

Xenia II (5)

Giving you my arm, I have gone down at least a million stairs
and now in your absence every step is a void.
Even so our long journey was soon over.
Mine lasts yet, but without the accompaniment
of bookings and connections, of the snares
and the shames of one who believes
the world is what he perceives.

I have gone down a million stairs, giving you my arm
not, surely, to prove four eyes might beat two.
I went down them with you because I knew
that of our pupils, yours, dimmed as they were,
only yours were true.

['Ho sceso...']

Attila József

Attila József, believe me, I am very fond of you, this has come
    down to me from my mother, she was goodness itself, she
    brought me into the world
It is no use comparing life to a shoe or a dry-cleaner's, there are
    other reasons why we love it
Redeem the world three times a day and cannot strike a match?
    if that is all they can do I am finished with them
How good it would be to buy a ticket and travel to Oneself, it is
    there all right, alive, inside us
Every morning I wash my thoughts in cold water, then they
    become brisk and bold
Diamonds, planted beneath our heart, can nurture good warm
    songs
Some people are pedestrian even on horseback, in cars, in planes,
    I can loll at dawn and listen to larks, yet I have crossed the
    chasm
We must look after our real souls as carefully as our best clothes,
    and keep them clean to celebrate the feast-days in.

['József Attila']

ATTILA JÓZSEF

Heart-Innocent

Without father, without mother, alone
without cradle, without shroud I go
without God, without land and home,
without kiss, without girl to know.

Three days and nothing to eat,
bite or banquet, fat or lean!
My twenty years, my strength and speed –
who'll buy this twenty-year machine?

And if no buyer comes – well then
I'll sell these years to the devil of hell!
become pure thief, heart-innocent,
yes, and be a killer as well!

They'll catch me, hang me like a lout,
lay me out in holy ground.
From then on my heart'll be proud –
death fattens the grass growing round.

['Tiszta szívvel']

118

ATTILA JÓZSEF

Mother

All this last week I have been thinking
of my mother, thinking of her taking
up in her arms the creaking basket
of clothes, without pausing, up to the attic.

Oh I was full of myself in those days –
shouting and stamping, crying to her to leave
her washing to others, to take me in place
of the basket, play with me under the eaves –

But calmly she went on, lifting out the clothes,
hanging them to dry, she had no time to scold
or even to glance at me, and soon the line
was flying in the wind, white and clean.

I cannot shout now – how could she hear?
I see her, great, vast, yet somehow she is near.
The wet sky shines washed with her blue,
her grey hair streams where the clouds scud through.

['Mama']

Meditative

Storm

If you've seen a child seizing a cockroach,
that's how I nipped it, two fingers closed
under its arm, muttering: So the storm's here!
And its tiny lightnings scrabbled at the air.

Mulberry-tree

An ancient mulberry stands at the roadside,
thick-set, stocky, like a country wet-nurse.
Driver, sir, watch out! it has an iron hide!
But oh, beggarman, its fruits are soft to crush.

Christian

Fat sheaves all round me, I waste in hunger,
    stroked and stroked by sorrow.
Bright are the sky's stars I stand under,
    like a crown of thorns.
Does this make me a Christian, however grudging?
    Only if there are no wars.

Punctuation-mark

All this is a game, you know. I'm writing here
in pencil. Gentry's money paid the paper.
These letters have no machine-gun rat-tat-tat
yet. Like poverty they gouge, like lice they bite.

['Tünödö']

ATTILA JÓZSEF

Unemployed

Eighteen months now
the bird can't rise from the ground.

In submarine market-caves
I've stumbled under slippery crates.

Been with the Danube shipping,
a strangler's grip on the cold rigging.

Had a hawker's, not a reader's view
of Móricz, Barbusse, Zola, Cocteau, Shaw...

Sold golden bread, then
watched it eaten, but still kept thin.

No bacon, no stove. Night on the benches
and grassy places – with the angels.

['Állás nélkül']

ATTILA JÓZSEF

Keep Going!

Mandarins hanged in Peking,
the dead man liked his cocaine.
– Go to sleep, you're rustling the straw.
The dead man liked his cocaine.

What does the poor man watch
through the window? Till and cash.
– Go to sleep, you're rustling the straw.
Through the window? Till and cash.

Buy yourself sausage and bread,
keep hardy, keep your head.
– Go to sleep, you're rustling the straw.
Keep hardy, keep your head.

You'll find the woman of gold,
she'll cook and never scold.
– Go to sleep, you're rustling the straw.
She'll cook and never scold.

['Biztató (Kínában...)']

ATTILA JÓZSEF

My Mother

She would hold the mug in both hands,
one Sunday as evening approached
she smiled in her own peaceful way
and sat a moment in the half dark –

A small saucepan held the supper
she brought home from the fine folks' house,
we went to bed, and I lay thinking
how they had a whole pot to devour –

This was my mother, tiny, early dead,
a washerwoman's lot is to die early,
her legs shake from the loads she carries,
her head throbs as she bends ironing –

And her mountains are the dirty washing!
She has a tranquillizing cloudscape
of steam, and as for pastures new
the washerwoman has the attic –

She pauses with the iron: I see her.
Her brittle body was broken by
capital, grew thin, grew thinner –
think about it, proletarians –

She was bent, you know, bent from washing,
I never knew how young she was,
she wore a clean apron in her dreams,
and the postman greeted her then –

['Anyám']

123

. . . .

It isn't me you hear crying, it's a growl from the earth.
Look out – the devil has lost his head – look out!
Crouch in the belly of the well –
squeeze against the window-pane –
hide behind the flash of diamonds –
beneath stones – in a swarm of flies –
oh, hide in the bread just drawn from the oven –
you, Poorman:
soak into the earth with a thunder-shower!
To plunge your face into yourself – wasted labour,
you are only washed in the waters of others.
Slip into a grass-blade: on its vein
you will stretch farther than the axis of this world.

O birds and foliage, machines and stars,
our sterile mother implores and reclaims her children.
So, Poorman, so –
and is this dreadful, or is it wonderful? –
it isn't me you hear crying, it's a growl from the earth.

['Nem én kiáltok...']

ATTILA JÓZSEF

Ode

1

Here I sit on a shining wall.
The light young summer wind
rises like the warm welcome of supper.
I accustom my heart to the silence:
not hard.
Here
I regain what I lost,
I bend my head,
my head hangs down.

My eyes are on the mane of the mountains –
your splendid brow,
every leaf on fire!
On the street no one, no one;
I see your skirt lifted by the wind.
Your hair strays under fine leaves,
I see your soft breasts
trembling –
as Szinva brook runs down –
Oh what I see:
a magic laugh
shining on your teeth,
on the round white stones.

2

Oh how I love you!
You have been able to force
speech from the universe –
and from solitude, weaving its fitful deceits
in the heart's deepest place.
Now, as the booming leaves the waterfall,
you leave, you run subdued, until
I cry from among the peaks of life, singing
in those distances hung between earth and heaven,
that I love you, that it is you,
sweet and suffering creature, that I love.

3

I love you as the child loves its mother,
as the silent cave loves its depths.
I love you as rooms love sunlight,
as the soul loves warmth and the body rest.
I love you as mortal men love living
and strive in its arms till death.

I am the watcher of your words, your smiles,
your moments – everything, as the earth watches
everything that falls.
My instincts, like acid on metal, shall
be engraved on your mind; my existence
takes form at last, dear love, from your sweet essence.

Loudly the moments pass by;
dumb you remain, dumb, and I
have ears for you alone.
Glittering stars – already they are setting,
but you are always steady in my sight.
Breath of silence in the cave: your flavour
stings cold in the mouth; at times your hand
with its delicate veining will bend
mistily round the glass of water.

4

Oh but what substance am I made of,
moulded and carved by your simplest glance?
What mind, what light and miracle
that can make me reach the gentle
dales of your fertile
body, through the mist of absence?

As the word is released by reason,
I can delve into your enigmas!...

Your veins quiver like bushes,
ceaselessly, bushes of roses.
They move in the undying stream,
for love to flourish in your face
and your belly to bear its fruit.

126

The sensitive soil of your flesh
is sown with finest roots,
thin threads it knots, unknots, –
for the juices of the tiny cells
to crowd to a growing mass,
and the leafy bush of the lungs
to murmur up its praise!

And the deep undying matter advances
singing in its galleries, and rich life emerges
from tireless wells, from the very scourings
of buried pits, of burning kidneys!

In you, the swelling hills
rise, constellations wink,
lakes move, and workshops work:
a million beings, quick
insects,
bladderwrack,
cruelty and goodness;
suns shine, auroras go dark –
here, in your huge essence,
the eternal unconscious wanders.

5

Like clotted blood, in shreds,
these words
are dropped in your path.
Existence stammers:
only law has a clear voice.
My active senses, reborn day after day,
are ready even now
for silence.

But up to now everything cries aloud –
chosen out of two thousand millions,
you alone, you the living bed,
you the gentle cradle, you the fierce tomb:
into yourself: into yourself I
beseech you, receive me.

(How deep the sky at daybreak!
Armies shine in light of steel.
The glitter hurts my sight.
I am lost, in this air.
Surely my heart must break,
beating in the light.)

6   *After-song*

(The train takes me, I follow after you,
perhaps today I'll find you again,
perhaps my burning face will be cool,
perhaps you'll say, in your undertone:

The water's lukewarm, go and try it!
A towel for your body, dry it!
The meat is baked, end your hunger!
In my bed for ever linger.)

['Óda']

ATTILA JÓZSEF

'On the pavement . . .'

On the pavement a small puddle gave a wink,
the shadows settled down upon the city
and all the cheeping swarming sparrows fixed
their claws in branches silently but firmly,
for anyone who sleeps must clutch more tightly
than people moving off in the waking world,
men and women, tramcars, revving taxis
milled around like the instincts and the mind.

Under a gateway I kissed a girl's mouth
and was soon lost melting into the crowd,
only to leave them, to make this poem flout
my cares and leave them, turn and turn about.
I brooded slowly to give it its shape,
my animal grief has all that human sense
of sadness which can recognize its face
in garish streets, in worse advertisements.

['A kövezeten']

ATTILA JÓZSEF

I Open the Door

I open the door. The congealed smell
of vegetables drifts slowly from
the kitchen which is filled, swept
through by the clawed stove's grin. The room

is empty, nobody. Sixteen years
ago, what I can never forget.
I sat on an oilskin-covered chair
in the kitchen, tried to whimper, could not.

I know very well my mother is gone,
but this absence gives me no rest,
and I know nothing. Am I a grown man?
(The washing-up bowl shows no rust.)

It doesn't hurt, but I was even unable
to touch her, I never saw her dead,
never cried. And it's incomprehensible
that this is what I see, for ever, ahead.

['Ajtót nyitok']

ATTILA JÓZSEF

Everything's Old

Everything's old here, the hoary storm
leans on a twisted stick of lightning,
trails through the thorn-bearded roses, piping,
with twig legs like theirs, tottering along.

Everything's old. Revolution
coughs as it crouches on sharp-edged stones
ready for pelting, and with hands all bones
holds a bright penny: my best creation.

Can I not have an old see-through hand,
so that I could trace my wrinkled brow,
lay my hand in my lap, and seem to show
that tears of mine were dropping to the ground?

My days of youth! that holy age!
Oho, I'm a frisky chilly fish
flung by flame into the twilight's dish,
my dying ash becoming weed and sedge.

['Öreg minden']

ATTILA JÓZSEF

They'd Love Me

I don't meditate on good and evil.
I work, and I suffer: that's all.

I make screw-propeller boats, crockery,
badly in bad times, well in ordinary.

Numberless my works! Only my love,
being aware of them, takes stock of them, my love

takes stock of them all, my love has faith
but is silent before creed or oath.

Make me a tree, and the crow, I believe,
would only nest if there was no tree near.

Make me a field, and the old farmer's hoe
will turn up nothing but the weeds I've grown.

You'd have to water potatoes with sweat
to see them thrive on my thankless earth.

I'm water? A marsh begins to form.
Fire? I'm ash. But if I was transformed

to a god, in place of the god they know,
men would love me in truth, with all their soul.

['Szeretnének']

ATTILA JÓZSEF

My Mother Washing Clothes a Wreath

My mother's dead now I don't know what to do with her
she held the mug in both hands
one Sunday at dusk she smiled gently
flowers came the name unregistered the porter never saw him
if it was China she lived in they would dispatch her to the dragons
but she stands up
far from me is the dragon now I'll hurry home for a handful of rice
and I will plait my wreath instead of you

she patched my coat saw how good I looked naked
nobody ever yet saw me naked
her laundering had stooped her permanently
I never realized what a young woman she was
in her dreams she had a white apron the postman touched his cap
      to her then.

['Anyam a mosásban gyászkoszorú']

ATTILA JÓZSEF

Dead Landscape

The water smokes, the bulrushes
sag and wilt into the wilderness.
The sky cowers deep in its quilt.
Thick silence cracks in the snow-filled
    field.

Gross and greasy the silent sundown;
flat the plain, featureless and round.
Only a single barge, heard
slapping self-absorbed on the furred
    lake.

Newborn time rattles in the cold
branches of the icy wood.
Chittering frost finds some moss here,
ties up its skeletal horse here
    to rest.

Then the vines. And among them plums.
Damp straw on the stocks and stumps.
And a procession of thin stakes,
good for old peasants' walking-sticks
    in the end.

A croft – this countryside revolves
all round it. Winter with its claws
keeps cracking plaster till it falls
in pieces from the homestead walls:
    cat's-play.

The pigsty door gapes wide open.
It sags and creaks, the wind's playpen.
What if a sucking-pig trots in
and a field of corn should sport and spin
    on the cob!

The room small, the peasants small.
Dried leaves in the smoker's bowl.
For these ones, no prayer will work.
They sit there, deep in the dark,
    thinking.

The vines are freezing for the landlord.
His is the crackling of the wood.
His is the pond and under its ice
it is for him the good fish hides
    in the mud.

['Holt vidék']

ATTILA JÓZSEF

The Woodcutter

I wade through the fresh timber-piles.
Sap-wood shines in the sun and cries.
My winged hair is powdered with cold.
Winter draws its nail on my neck.
Time passes with a velvet step.

Everything sparkles: the freeze-up like an axe,
the land, our brows, the sky, our eyes.
And from the jet of shavings where the day
breaks out, another woodcutter growls:
Bite the trunk deep, we don't want frills!

Break down the oaks without a word!
Why be a laggard if the tree should bleed?
Strike the trunk, strike the doomed wood,
the feudal puszta groans and howls!
– says the axe, the broad axe, as it smiles.

['Favágó']

136

ATTILA JÓZSEF

Blighty Numbers

Farmworker-feet first
Amputated from the spade...Nothing now
Of the warm colour-drizzle to soak
The dryness of their eyes.

Clamour of bell-metal
Moulted into satanic tanks
Smashed their fine spine-steel
Into grenades.

Infiltrated lungs are
Marched through by gasping froth-fiends
And whole Siberias were interned
In their gentle brains.

These are the ones
Whose mothers received just something back
At the customs-post of more human pits
Where now all kinds of

Stammering Christs are
Calcifying into one, till the bacchanalia
Of death-rattles mounts up into a
Terror-sermon on the mount.

On their missing arms
The breadwinning palm is fixed as a fist,
It sears their heart, it rings out
The advent of Peace.

['Rokkantak']

ATTILA JÓZSEF

March 1937

Soft rain is drifting like a smoke
across the tender fuzz of wheat.
As soon as the first stork appears
winter shrivels in retreat.
Spring comes, tunnelling a path
mined with exploding spikes of green.
The hut, wide open to the sun,
breathes hope and wood-dust sharp and clean.

The papers say that mercenaries
are ravaging the face of Spain.
A brainless general in China
chases peasants from hill to plain.
The cloth we use to wipe our boots
comes laundered back in blood again.
All round, big words bemuse and smooth
the voiceless miseries in men.

My heart is happy as a child's.
Flora loves me. But oh what arms
the beauty of love? For us, for all,
war stirs its withering alarms.
The bayonet contends in zeal
with the assaulting tank. Alone
I draw to us the force I need
against the fear I can't disown.

Men – women – all have sold themselves.
A heart? They keep it close as sin.
Hearts torn by hate – I pity you,
I shudder to see hatred win.
A little life on earth I have,
yet here I watch all life unfold –
O Flora, in this blaze of love
nothing surrenders to the cold!

May our daughter be beautiful
and good, our son be fearless, keen.
May they transmit some sparks beyond
star-clusters you and I have seen.
When this sun loses its great fire,
the children of our illumination
will launch towards infinity
their own galactic exploration.

['Marcius']

ATTILA JÓZSEF

Epitaph for a Spanish Farm-Hand

General Franco made me one of his crack troops,
    fear of the firing-squad ensured I was no deserter.
It was fear that kept me fighting justice and freedom
    at the walls of Irun. Death found me all the same.

['Egy spanyol földmíves sírverse']

140

ATTILA JÓZSEF

Elegy

Smoke, under a low leaden sky, swirls hooded
in thick banks over the sad land:
and so my soul, back and forward,
sways like the smoke.
Sways, yet stays.

Iron soul you are – yet tender in images!
Going behind the heavy tread of the real,
look deep into yourself, see
where you were born!

– Here, under a sky once supple and flowing
across the loneliness of thin dividing
walls, where the menacing, impassively imploring silence
of misery slowly loosens the melancholy
so solidly
packed in the thinker's heart
and mingles it with the heart
of millions.

The whole dominion of men
begins here. Here everything is a ruin.
A tough euphorbia has spread
its umbrella over the abandoned factory yard.
Into a damp darkness
the days go down by stained steps
from shatter of paltry windows.
Tell me:
is it here you are from?
Here, where you are tied to your gloomy wish
to be like other wretched souls
in whom this age, the great age, is
straitjacketed: the others whose faces
are marked by every line that's made?

Here you rest, here where the rickety creak
of a fence still guards the greed
of the moral order,
and watches it all.
Can you recognize yourself? Here the souls
wait in a void for the towering beauty-filled
future, as the dark and desolate shacks
have dreams of houses, lifting high
a nimble web of murmurs. Set
in the dried mud, fragments of glass
stare with fixed eyes, cut off from the light,
over the tortured meadow-grass.

From the low hills a thimble
of sand rolls down at random...and there's a flash,
a buzz of some fly – black, green, or blue –
attracted here from richer neighbourhoods
by the rags,
by the leavings of man.
Good is mother earth, tormented in her care,
also in her way
preparing a table.
A yellow weed springs in a saucepan there!

What have you to say
to this dry heart's-leap of recognition which draws me –
to a landscape that is bone of my bone?
What of my rich torment – coming back, back here?
So a mother's son,
after the cudgels of strangers, will return.
Here, only here, you may smile and cry, and
here, here only, can your sinew endure,
my soul! This is my native land.

['Elégia']

142

ATTILA JÓZSEF

Profit

Pound your dough by the gas-flame,
or bake your red bricks with their cavities;
get the hoe to shatter your palm;
sell yourself as your skirt twists;
floor a mine-shaft, crawl the pits;
shoulder a sack through the markets;
learn a trade or don't learn it –
here you stand, there profit sits.

Rinse your silks in a petrol-stream;
pick onions, squatting in the grit;
kill the goat that bleats your name;
cut trouser-cloth to tailor's fit;
stick with it! Why should you stop it?
You'll get the sack, for what good that is!
Then beg? Or burgle? But laws hit –
here you stand, there profit sits.

Wring out verse in a lovelorn dream;
cure Prague ham for festivities;
cull herbs; sweat at the coal-seam;
keep ledgers, cover up their secrets;
wear caps with gold braid on the skip;
live in Paris or in Claypitts –
even with wages in your pocket
here you stand, there profit sits.

Attila, I could go on and bore you;
you know you don't live on salmon cuts –
you can hang about or they can employ you
but here you stand, there profit sits.

['Haszon']

143

ATTILA JÓZSEF

'Freight trains shunt . . .'

Freight trains shunt on the tracks,
the dreamlike clanking
fits light shackles
on the silent landscape.

The broken stones
crouch in their own shadow,
glitter in
secret, show
they are in place
as never before.

Unknown the enormous night
this heavy night is but a shaving of,
as it drops down on us
like an iron splinter on dust.

Sun-born desire!
If the bed holds a shadow, would you tire
of lying awake
through the weight
of that whole night?

The freight shed
has a dusty lamp burning nearby
which shows itself but nothing else.
The mind in its longing is like this.
It flickers bravely, against
the great dead
light of the sky.

['Tehervonatok tolatnak . . .']

144

ATTILA JÓZSEF

Night in the Suburbs

The light smoothly withdraws
its net from the yard, and as water
gathers in the hollow of the ditch,
darkness has filled our kitchen.

Silence. – The scrubbing-brush sluggishly
rises and drags itself about;
above it, a small piece of wall is in
two minds to fall or not.

The greasy rags of the sky
have caught the night; it sighs;
it settles down on the outskirts;
it sets off through the square, going where?
It kindles a dim moon for a fire.

The workshops stand
like a ruin;
within
the thickest gloom
a plinth for silence to assume.

On the windows of the textile factory
the bright moon now climbs
in a cluster of light,
the moon's soft light
is a thread at the boards of the looms,
and all through the idle night
the darkened machines weave the dreams
of the weaver-girls – the unravelled dreams.

Farther on, iron-works, nut-and-bolt-works
and cement-works, bounded by a graveyard.
Family vaults alive with echoes.
The factories sleep with their arms over
the sombre secret of their resurrection.
A cat comes poking a paw through the railings.

145

The superstitious watchman catches
a will-o-the-wisp – a flash of
brilliance – the cold
glitter of beetle-backed dynamos.

A train-whistle.

The damp explores the greyness,
probes the leaves of splintered trees,
lays the dust more heavily
along the streets.

On the street a policeman, a muttering workman.
A comrade rushes down
with leaflets in his hand:
sniffs ahead like a dog,
looks over his shoulder like a cat,
the lamp-posts watch him pass.

The tavern mouth ejects a sour glare;
puddles vomit from the window-sill;
the lamp inside shakes, gasping for air.
A solitary labourer stares.
The host is asleep, he snores.
The other one grinds his teeth by the wall,
his wretchedness gushes and weeps down the stair.
He hymns the revolution still.

The water cracks, goes stiff
like chilled metal, the wind
wanders about like a dog,
its huge tongue dangles
as it slobbers up the water.
Swimming like rafts on the stream
of the voiceless night, paillasses –

The warehouse is a grounded boat,
the foundry an iron barge,
while the foundryman sees a pink baby
taking shape in the iron mould.

Everything wet, everything heavy.
A musty hand maps the countries
of misery. There, on the barren fields,
on ragged grass – paper, and rags.
If only the paper could fly up! It stirs
slightly, weakly. See it try
to get on its way...

Filthy sheets are fluttering around
in your slapping wind, your wetting wind,
O night!
You cling to the sky as unthreaded
cambric clings to the rope, as sadness
clings to life, O night!
Night of the poor! Be my coal,
and the smoke at my heart's core,
cast me in your ore,
make me a seamless forge,
and make me a hammer that labours and rings,
and make my blade strike till it sings,
O night!

Grave night, heavy night.
My brothers, I too must turn out the light.
May misery be a brief lodger in our soul.
May the lice leave our body whole.

['Külvárosi éj']

ATTILA JÓZSEF

'Well, in the end I have found my home...'

Well, in the end I have found my home,
the land where flawless chiselled letters
guard my name above the grave
where I'm buried, if I have buriers.

It will take me like a collecting-box,
this earth. For no one (sadly) wants
wartime leftovers of base metal,
wretched devalued iron coins.

Or an iron ring engraved
with noble words: new world, rights, land.
Our laws are still the fruit of war;
gold rings shine finer on the hand.

For many years I was alone.
Then all about me was a crowd.
It's up to you, they said, although
I'd have loved to follow them round.

It was like that, empty, the way I lived:
no one has to tell me it was.
I was compelled to play the fool
and now I die without a cause.

In that whole whirlwind of my life
I have tried to stand my ground.
More sinned against than sinning, I
leave that thought and laugh aloud.

Spring is beautiful, summer too,
autumn better, winter the best
when you leave your hopes for family
and hearth to other men at last.

['Ime, hát megleltem hazámat...']

148

ATTILA JÓZSEF

In Light, White Clothes
To Paul Ignotus

I have chewed it all and spat it out,
everything that is not my food.
Up there, I neither care nor doubt:
soap-bubble or empyrean vault?
I know what is and is not good.

And like a little child, I know
only playing brings happiness.
I have so many games to show;
reality always turns to go,
appearance lives in steadiness.

The rich can have no love for me
as long as I am poor like this.
And the poor, I leave them equally
cold, how could I be consolatory
where love comes shameful and amiss?

I am the creator of my own love...
Star and planet feel my tread:
I set out for the gods above,
in opposition – heart calm enough –
in light, white clothes striding ahead.

['Könnyü, fehér ruhában']

Mozart: Cassation 1

To S. Gubaidulina

   mozart divine mozart straw compasses
divine blade wind paper infarct mother-of-god
wind jasmine operation wind divine mozart
cassation twig jasmine operation angel
divine rose straw heart cassation mozart

['Motsart: Kassatsiya 1']

A Note: Apophatic

K.B.

but the night of this world should have been
enormous terrifying like the Lord-not-Revealed
such a thing could be endured
but murder-people
have seeped into the darkness of this white night:
terrifyingly-simple
terrifying Moscow night

['Zapis': apophatic']

GENNADY AIGI

Lake and Bird

The lake – so ravishingly-irregularly-round, so
distantly-translucent, that our appearance before this
is virtually a reverence.

But in the very middle of it – on an unseen rock? –
is a bird: it trembles, flutters its wings, trembles –
and does not fly away, – and it is like: this place
was always so and always will be so.

Suddenly – nothing but Sun. Happiness of Immensity.
And – with a single sigh-of-existence:

'Amen'

['Ozero i ptitsa']

Field: Height of Winter
To René Char

god's-pyre! – this bright field
pushing everything right through (mile-posts and wind and distant
                                    dots of mills: more and more –
                                    as if out of this world – as if
                                    not in reality – withdrawn: o all
                                    this – unlacerating sparks
                                    flame of non-universal pyre)
I am – without tracks of whatever there may be
not universally shining
god's-pyre

['Pole: v razgare zimy']

GENNADY AIGI

KRCH – 80

(For the 80th anniversary of A.E. Kruchonykh)

o I am
your surface
burning invisibly
from the interface *I-am-not* –

to the poet a name
crunching creative:

krch

krch

krch

Sending Roses

to nephritic space
this greeting
of white! –

and let it ring out
there – as in an opal room
every roused velvetiness
with an eulenspiegelling of the stalk:

'till-till'

['Pri posylke roz']

GENNADY AIGI

Suburban House

To my son Konstantin

but from Homeland-Life
strange
secretive –

the soul
grows gold
in the window-frame:

the willow
flowers –

– the child
stammers! –

secret meeting (flowering and chatter) –

in your – unstained – Homeland

['Dom za gorodom']

GENNADY AIGI

The Birches Rustle

To V. Korsunsky

and I myself – murmuring:
'but maybe God . . .' –

birch-whisper:
'is dead . . .' –

and we
are the fallout – keeping it going? –

but why should it
not be like that? –

the dust howls up lonely and empty . . . –

(whisper of birches . . .
all living flesh murmurs . . .) –

and he will Resurrect
again? . . . –

. . . even without pain:

as for ever . . . –

the rustle – as from this! . . . –

. . . . ¯
(as if forsaken – rustle of autumn)

['Shumyat berezy']

154

GENNADY AIGI

Once More: Places in the Forest

again t h e y a r e b e i n g s u n g ! they are! again t h e y
are resounding – everywhere – in unison! –

again about that time
wakening-time:

brightly
– by-the-meadow-of-suffering! –
motionlessly
and clearly – endlessly! –
and as if the morning was unwavering
in me: as in the world: absolutely:

and there they placed that place
in the midst of others related
to them:

place I once knew! –

it shone
like an hour of happiness:

with a high
clear centre:

hawthorn – keeping silent beside the singing
like god keeping silent – behind the resounding Word:

keeping silent – with a personality untouched:

one touch – and that is: n o m o r e G o d

['Snova: mesta v lesu']

155

EZRA POUND

Lament of the Frontier Guard: A Restruction

Murnin o the Merches-Gaird

By the Nor'Yett, the wund blaws fu o saun,
Lanelie fae time's jizzen tae thir days!
The wid crines, the gress yallas at hairst.
I sclim tours an tours
        tae vizzy the barbour straths:
Oorie barmekin, the lift, the braid desart.
Nae waw stauns noo i this clachan.
Banes blanchit wi a thoosan forsts,
Hie-humphit deid-knoks, owrheildit wi trees an gress;
Wha brung uz thir effeirs?
Wha brung the levin o the cankert coorts?
Wha brung the airmy wi its touk an tarantara?
Barbour keengs.
A douce spring, cheengit tae bluid-gowpin hairst.
A stramash o fechters, spreed owr this haill kintra,
Three hunner an saxty thoosan,
An dool, dool lik dash an dag.
Dool awaw, an dool, dool at retour.
Toom, toom faulds,
Wi nae a chiel o the fecht upo them,
        Nae langer birkies tae gaird or tae breenge.
Och, hoo sall ye ken the doolie wae at the Nor'Yett,
Wi oor ledar Li Mu's name negleckit,
An uz, the gairdsmen, fother for teegers.

[Pound's poem is a translation from the Chinese of Li Po (701-762)]